A Random Life?

Leslie Newhouse

Published by Leslie Newhouse, 2022.

While every precaution has been taken in the preparation of this book, the publisher assumes no responsibility for errors or omissions, or for damages resulting from the use of the information contained herein.

A RANDOM LIFE?

First edition. February 18, 2022.

ISBN: 979-8215406700

Written by Leslie Newhouse.

Forward

My name is Leslie Newhouse. I practiced medicine for 41 years. In November of 2020, I lost the most important person in my life. The person for whom I would have gladly given my life. I lost my wife of 52 years. We had been together since we were sixteen years old. I loved her with all my heart and I fell apart. Shortly thereafter, is when the strange things started happening around the house. Things that I couldn't scientifically explain. I talked to Doctor Lamantia, a good friend, about the strange events. I showed her the two occurrences that I had videoed. She asked if there were more and I said yes, but these are the only ones I could actually document. She asked me to write the others down so she could read them. So, in March of 2021, when I was a complete mess, I reluctantly started writing. When completed, I had my wife's sisters, Sue and Linda, read the story and they encouraged me to think about publishing it, but that was never my intention. In the third week of February 2022, I was researching something on the internet and just randomly, totally out of place, a publishing company appeared in the list. On a whim, I emailed them the first paragraph to see if my writing was any good. They emailed me back the next day, instructing me go to their website, fill out permission forms, and please send them the rest of the story. Four days later, I received an email that they had evaluated, accepted the story and that they had submitted the story to other publishing companies that reviewed it, accepted it and were going to publish it. In print it's now on 17 different company websites and the E-book is on 18 worldwide. I didn't expect this. I wrote it with all the love I had in my heart, and I did my very best to explain all the strange things that were now happening in our home that I still can't scientifically explain. I was told that our story may have been accepted so quickly because other people, in similar situations, are now coming forward about things happening in their homes that they can't explain. This is a very unique positive love story. One that you would be very hard pressed to find another one quite like it. I still miss miss my wife immensely. I love her with all my heart, and this is our amazing story.

A Random Life?
"Love does not see with the eyes, but with the soul."
-William Shakespeare-

A Random Life?
"Love Never Dies"

Explanation

I am neither a writer nor a journalist. I have practiced medicine for the past 41 years. Twenty-nine years in the Emergency Room and Urgent Care along with twelve years in Cardio Thoracic Surgery. I am hoping to make this more like a conversation similar to that of your best friend confiding in you. It's a very unusual story. One that starts out normally but becomes one that I would have never expected to be a part of in my wildest dreams, but here I am. It is a story, with history, humor and medical stories with a love story woven throughout where love never dies. It will not finish in the way that it began, and I will never be the same.

A Love Story

This story starts out in November of 1948, in the small farming community of Osage, Iowa. In small Midwest towns in 1948 it was more common to be born at home than in a hospital if you had limited means. I was born in my grandparents' home so my grandmother could help after the delivery. Kindly old Doctor Doyle came to the house alone that day, did the delivery and left a bill for $50. The family I was born into was a very hard working, grounded, down to earth, matter of fact family. In 1948, 50 dollars was a great deal of money to them. It was half a month's wages or more for some. My mother, laughingly, told me recently it was a cold dreary Saturday afternoon in November, and she didn't have anything else to do so she decided to give birth. That statement gives you a proper insight into my mother's personality. My mother was a unique individual that projected a very hard exterior and appeared tough but within that hard exterior beat a very soft compassionate heart for children. Which she managed to keep covered up quite well. She grew up during the depression when times were difficult and life was hard. My grandmother would save and dye animal feed sacks different colors and sew them into dresses for my mother and her sister to wear. They raised and canned all of their own food. My grandfather hunted for meat and sold the hides for what money he could get. He also worked for the WPA, a government work program, for 50 cents a day when he could work and when they had work. My mother said that she never thought of themselves as poor because so many others in that town were in the same situation. She was thankful that they were self-sufficient and never had to go hungry like many people in the cities did. No bread lines or soup kitchens were needed. People would help each other out as much as they could. They were your neighbors and your friends. In Osage they would survive or perish together. My father's story was very similar except for the feed sacks.

My mother celebrated her 16th birthday two months before I was born. I was extremely fortunate because my parents had decided to get married in April of 1948 after they found out my mother was pregnant. In those days pregnant girls had two options, get married or sent off to what they called "Homes for Unwed Mothers." Girls would quietly disappear, usually at night, to stay at these homes until they were ready to give birth. There was one of these homes across the street from the University of Iowa Hospital. It was a two story brick building that was the old unused nurse's residence. At delivery time, the girls would be placed in wheel chairs and secretly rushed through underground tunnels that passed under the street and into the hospital to give birth. Then they would return home alone with the story that they had been ill and had gone away for treatment. It happened often enough that people knew what it meant. The girls would be treated by some in the community as if they wore an imaginary "Scarlet Letter on their chest." But it allowed the girl's parents to at least pretend that nothing had happened.

After I was born, we moved into a house on main street that had been converted into upstairs and downstairs apartments. We lived upstairs and, down stairs lived a little girl with her older sister and parents. When we were old enough, our parents would have us spend time playing together because we were the same age and we got along very well. I don't remember this time in our lives, we were much too young. That little girl that lived downstairs was destined to become the absolute love of my life, and her name was Donette. As humans, we are imperfect at best. So, it may not be perfect, but it is what I was told and how I remember living it from my perspective. Memories have a tendency to change and soften with time. They can sometimes become what you wish they were. All I can do is promise to do my best. This is our story and it is dedicated to our children and grandchildren. So, they will know who we were and what made us the people we became.

I was named after my father's oldest brother, Leslie, who at the age of 11 was thrown from a startled horse and suffered a few minor bruises and small a cut from a rusty barbed wire fence to his arm. It was a small but deep linear cut that the doctor didn't think needed stitches, it was bandaged and it shouldn't be a problem. But that cut festered and Leslie later died. He suffered in excruciating pain from the unrelenting constant muscle spasms of tetanus. Think of the worst Charlie Horse you have ever had in the calf muscle of your leg, a muscle spasm that made you cry out in pain. Then multiply that times your entire body and it doesn't go away. The spasms are so strong that they can tear tendons away from the bone and ultimately destroy your ability to take a breath. He died at home. I can't imagine what my father and my grandparents went through listening and watching this horrific ordeal.

My father was a tall slender man who had enlisted in the Navy as a teenager just before the beginning of World War II in the Pacific. He was aboard a naval ship that was three days from arriving at Pearl Harbor when he received orders to return to San Francisco to put a Merchant Marine ship into service. He was transferred at sea via a bosuns chair. A board suspended on a single rope over the water to another ship on its way to California. Three days later Pearl Harbor was attacked. We don't know the fate of the original ship he was on. He said he heard a rumor later in the war that it had gone down with all hands aboard after being struck by a Japanese torpedo. My father fought the Japanese from a gun turret on the bow of the Merchant Marine ship that he helped put into service. It carried supplies, ammunition and an occasional fighter airplane to the fighting in the pacific. He would never talk about the war until much later in life. The first time I remember him saying anything about it, he was over 80 years of age. He told me about fighting Japanese Zeros, shooting down Kamikazes, and avoiding the Japanese ship convoys. He said one moon lit night when he was walking deck watch on the bow. He saw a torpedo on collision course with his ship. At the very last minute it suddenly veered off and crossed in front of the ship's bow. He watched it go by and then disappear. It happened so fast he didn't have time to react. On its collision course it would have struck the very spot where he was standing. My father looked down and didn't say anything for a few moments. To this day he doesn't know why that torpedo turned, but he was very thankful that it did. He smiled, then told me about his trip from San Francisco by ship all the way around the world to New York City. Then he traveled by train across country back to San Francisco and a new ship. He was so proud of that complete circumnavigation of the entire world. Then his eyes would tear up, and he would tell me about the day, near the end of the war, when they picked up the emaciated American prisoners of war. Many of whom couldn't walk and were nothing more than skin and bones. They had been rescued from a Japanese prisoner of war camp and had to be helped or carried aboard. That vision stayed with him for all of those years and was the main reason he tried not to remember. I am very proud of my father to this day.

When I was three, we moved to Pomona California, just outside of Los Angeles. My father could play guitar and had a very nice singing voice. I believe he had dreams of breaking into the music business and that was the reason we had moved. He loved country and western music, and his favorite singer was Hank Williams. I remember only bits and pieces from our short time there. We lived in an upstairs apartment, that we had to go all the way to the back of the house and climb the outside unpainted wooden stairs that would give me slivers in my bare feet or hands. My mother would sit on top me to hold me down while she would dig those slivers out with a sewing needle. I would scream and cry. She would say, "Shut up and hold still or I will give you something to really cry about." I thought that was what this was. I remember there was an olive tree in the front yard, and that olives picked off the tree tasted horrible. They didn't taste like the olives that came out of a jar and I would spit them out. There was an older couple that owned the house and lived downstairs. They were nice people and I remember liking them. They were like grandparents.

My mother was young and had never been away from her home and family. She always put on a tough brave face, but one evening my father returned home from work and couldn't find her. She was in the bedroom, out of sight, sitting on the closet floor with the door closed, crying. She had just found out she was pregnant and very much wanted to be home with family. The older couple, that owned the house, were sad that we were leaving but understood why we had to go. We loaded up the car and moved back to Osage after just one year in California. We moved into an older small three-bedroom house close to my grandparents. Osage was a cute little town with a maple tree lined main street, parks and a large outdoor swimming pool. It had a population of around 3500 people and one old grouch that lived next door to us who delighted in scaring little children. The neighborhood children were all afraid of him and dared not to touch a blade of his grass or we would be loudly scolded. In later years I tried to get to know him, but he wouldn't have it. I found him not to be mean or scary but just sad. His house was becoming somewhat run down. He never had any visitors that I ever noticed and he seemed to not like children for some reason. No one knew why exactly. Some people wondered where his wife was or if he ever had one. One rumor was that his wife had died in child birth, but it was just a rumor. When I was eleven, we heard from a neighbor that he had died in the hospital from diabetes. I didn't know what that was. My mother told me it was from eating too much sugar. I certainly didn't want that, but I wanted to know how much was too much. It started me wondering. That night after I went to bed, my father came upstairs. He asked, "Is everything alright? You've been awfully quiet today." I said, "When will I die? I'm named after your brother. He died when he was eleven. I'm eleven. Am I going to die?" Dad smiled and said, "That has nothing to do with you. That was just an accident. You're going to live for a very long time and you're going to be just fine." I felt reassured, but I asked, "What happens when we die?" He replied while tucking me in, "I don't know. No one has ever come back to tell us." I said, "But you're a grown up. You're supposed to know all the answers." He laughed and said, "I hate to tell you this, but grownups don't know all the answers. Only the questions. It's late. You need to close your eyes and go to sleep. See you in the morning. Good night."

In those days people didn't lock their home doors and they left their keys in their car. No one worried about break-ins or robberies. The worst that would happen would be a person that stumbled out of the bar and wandered into the wrong house. You would take them by the hand, lead them outside and point them in the direction of their house. Give them a slight push to get them started and they would stumble on home. They were your neighbors, and you watched out for them. There was a person that lived down the road from us named Ding. I don't know if that was his real name but that is what he went by. He had lost his driver's license for drunk driving and now traveled by much safer cart and horse. That horse was his faithful partner that took him to work and home every day. Every Friday night at bar closing time, after an evening of playing cards and consuming alcohol with friends, people would help Ding or sometimes carry Ding out to the horse cart. They would place him in the cart, pat the horse on the rump and his faithful horse, who knew the route, would automatically slowly ploddingly take sleeping Ding home. Neighbors would check on him to make sure he got into the house and he didn't spend the night in the horse cart asleep. In the winter they would put his horse away in the barn so it wouldn't spend the night outside in the cold and snow. In small towns in the 1950s, there was a kindness that ran through most of the community and that was just how life was in a small town in Iowa.

When I was 5 years old, my mother lied to me. She said, "Let's go to the drive-in and get some ice cream." That sounded good to me. She placed my sister who was one year old in the back seat and I got in the front, but we didn't go to the drive-in. We parked in front of Doctor Huber's office on main street. Past experience had taught my mother she had to act quickly. She jumped out of the car picked up my sister, ran into the office, handed my sister to the nurse and raced back to the car but it was too late. Cars didn't have power steering in those days. They had huge steering wheels. I knew where we were and what it meant. I had intertwined my arms and legs through the steering wheel and was holding on for dear life. Doctor Huber was our family doctor. Every time I was taken there, I got a shot of something. Every spring we had to get a polio shot. If you were ill, no matter what you had, you got a painful shot of penicillin. I remember when he came to our house once, because I was very sick in bed with the measles and he bent the needle in my hip giving me a shot of penicillin. I hated doctors and they smelled funny.

My mother tried to talk me out, then tried to pull me out with no success. My arms and legs were intertwined in that steering wheel tight and terror makes you very strong. Today she may have been arrested for what happened next but probably not. I got the worst paddling I have ever had, yanked out of the car kicking and screaming. She dragged me into the waiting room by my left arm, still kicking and screaming, where they immediately took us to the farthest exam room in the back of the building. Doctor Huber walked in with two nurses who held me down. My mother grabbed my arm and held it tight. Doctor Huber snapped a small glass tube in half, scratched the skin on my shoulder with one end of the tube, put a drop of liquid from the tube on the scratch and covered it with a band aid, then said, "We're done." I stopped screaming, looked at the band aid and said, "That didn't hurt." I looked at my mother whose face was bright red, and I knew I was in trouble. When we got back in the car, my mother just sat there holding onto the steering wheel and staring out the windshield for some time. I was sitting in the front seat up against the car door trying to be as far away from her as I could. I was trying to make myself as small and inconspicuous as possible. I knew that I had embarrassed her. I dare not say a word and draw her attention. She then turned her head toward me and in a low voice she calmly said, "You know I can kill you and make another one just like you. No jury of mothers would ever convict me." She started the car and drove home. I never did that again and there was no ice cream.

Osage had one school system but two elementary schools. One on the north side of town and one on the south side. Donette went to the north one and I attended the one on the south side. In first grade I spent an entire day sitting in the "cloakroom" because I pointed out to my teacher, Miss Parks who had white hair and I thought was ancient, that no one wore cloaks. It should be called the coatroom. It seemed perfectly obvious to me, but the rest of the class continued to do what Miss Parks wanted and called it the cloakroom. I couldn't understand what was wrong with them. Couldn't they see? I spent several more days during the school year sitting in the "cloakroom" because I called it what the facts told me it was, a coatroom. It was where we hung up our coats, not cloaks. If someone told me the bird, I was looking at was a duck, but I knew it was a goose. Why would I call it a duck. This was the beginning of looking at the facts and thinking for myself. Not everything someone tells you is the truth, after all my own mother said we were going to get ice cream.

Osage was a great place to grow up. As kids, we could climb on our bicycles and ride anywhere in town, to the park, swimming pool, fishing at the Cedar River or on some great imaginary adventure that usually involved exploring for treasure, pirates, cowboys or monsters. We could spend the entire day at the swimming pool for a dime. We would get so sunburned at the beginning of summer and so tan by the end. I remember one particularly painful sunburn, that I should not have complained about. My uncle Ernie said he would fix it so it didn't hurt so badly. He had me take my shirt off and he then poured vinegar all over my bare back and shoulders. The pain from the vinegar on the sunburn was so severe that I became dizzy and almost passed out. When the pain from the vinegar wore off, the pain from the sunburn was mild in comparison. The sunburn hadn't changed, but I didn't mind the pain now. It was nothing compared to the pain from the vinegar. The perception of pain was all relative and never trust one who wants to pour vinegar on you.

No one ever worried about us as long as we were home by dinner. If you were late for dinner and food got burned or cold, you were in serious trouble. One evening I was quite late for dinner and when I walked in the door, I knew I was in trouble from the look on my mother's face. She asked why I was so late. I believed I had a good reason, I answered that I had an argument with someone that called us names and they were really bad names. My mother asked what the names were? I answered that I really didn't want to repeat them. My mother hesitated for a moment and then asked "Are you bleeding?" I thought that was a strange question and I answered, "No?" "Do you have any broken bones?" Again, I answered, "No?" Now I'm wondering where this was going. Am I about to have a broken bone? She sat down at the kitchen table across from me and said, "Then why do you care? They are just words. We know the truth. We know who we are. Words can only hurt you if you let them. When you allow them to affect you and change what you do or how you feel that person wins. They have accomplished what they set out to do. They are trying to impress someone, or belittle you in front of others which makes them feel more important. They got a reaction out of you tonight and that was what they wanted. When you gave them that reaction, you allowed them to win. You allowed this. You need to just shrug it off, act like it doesn't matter, which it doesn't and then say out loud, I don't care, you're a moron. Then walk away confidently without saying anything further. It will make them appear unimportant as if you don't think they are important enough to pay them any attention. What they just said will become unimportant to everyone they were trying to impress. It will mess with their mind and you will have just won." My parents had waited dinner for me, and we all sat down to eat. It was fried Spam again. This time sprinkled with brown sugar and crushed pineapple. It was a little over done, but it was a very good dinner that night for all of us. Later that evening, while lying in bed, I thought about what she said and that she may be right. I did what she told me to do and it did blow their minds. Soon everything changed. The name calling disappeared because it didn't get the reaction they wanted, but that wasn't the only change. I had changed also. There is a very good confident feeling you get inside when you no longer allow yourself to be a victim or feel like a victim. No one can take that feeling away from me, unless I let them. It's my life. I own it.

In 1942, shortly after Donette's father and mother Donald and Alice, were married, Don was drafted into the army. He was going to be sent overseas to Europe during World War II. He didn't want to leave his new bride and she didn't want him to go, but they had no choice. They had just gotten married and loved each other dearly. The thought of him going to war with the possibility they may never see each other again terrified them. After basic training, he was assigned to a team whose job was sneaking behind enemy lines to blow up bridges and cut off enemy supplies. Then rebuild the bridges and roads for our soldiers to use. Later in the war when destroying and rebuilding bridges wasn't needed any longer, he was reassigned to the motor pool as a mechanic. This is where he learned how to rebuild vehicles that had been blown up, shot full of holes and almost destroyed. While Don was gone, Alice lived in constant fear of seeing the man in the black suit, carrying a telegram in his hand, walking up the sidewalk to her front door. Everyone knew what that meant. Someone wasn't coming home. When that man in the black suit drove into the neighborhood, parked his car and got out. Someone would yell, "He's Here!" Everyone raced nervously to their front door and stood anxiously waiting to see which sidewalk he chose and terrified it would be theirs. When it happened to a neighbor, the neighborhood wept for her. The war had become all too real and Alice knew she could be next. None of us in the family knew any of this until years later when our daughter interviewed her grandfather and grandmother for her High School history class project about World War II. It was a total surprise. Don and Alice never once mentioned the war, and Don never thought of himself as a hero. He said he was just doing his job, and glad he was able to come home.

After the war, Donette's father was now a mechanic who owned his own shop. Everyone that knew him, knew him as Don. He was an absolute meticulous artist with tools. Don was the Rembrandt of restoring antique cars and trucks back to better than new condition. He and Donette had a very special bond between them and she was named after him. In Donette's eyes her father could do anything. One morning at 5 am, my father and I were on our way to work at the gas station when we were stopped at the main street stoplight. We were astounded to see an antique airplane with its wings taken off driving down the center of main street and crossing right in front of us with Donette's father at the controls. He was on his way from the airport to his shop to restore the aircraft. When it was completely restored, he drove it back. He once took two wrecked cars, a 1965 and a 1966 Mustang, cut them in half, then welded the undamaged front and back halves together. Don rebuilt it to perfect condition and that car was driven over 4000 miles all the way to California and back.

My grandparents lived on a small acreage, on the outside edge of Osage, in between where the town and farms met. They always had animals around such as chickens, ducks, geese, turkeys, horses, dogs and rabbits. You name it and they probably had it. My grandfather was quite a horse trader so some animals came and went. They were traded for the things that they really needed for the house, barn, garden or just for fun. My grandfather loved the art of the trade and out foxing another savvy trader. He particularly liked to trade for animals that had been abused and give them a good home or trade them to a good home where they would be well cared for. He traded for a beautiful shiny coated black stallion named Rickey, a black three-quarter Hackney mare named Beauty and an ornery Shetland pony named Dolly. Like in the story, "Black Beauty," Rickey and Beauty had been abused. The other trader that owned Rickey thought he had out foxed and put one over on my grandfather. We found out later Rickey was a breath holder. When you would put a saddle on him, he would take a deep breath in to expand his chest and then hold his breath. The first time I tried to ride him, I tightened the sinch on the saddle to hold it in place, put my foot in the stirrup and got on. Rickey exhaled, the sinch became loose, he started bucking, the saddle fell under his belly and I was on the ground. I thought I had not tightened the sinch tight enough. I did it again only this time tighter, with the same result, and I was on the ground. When we tried to put a saddle on Beauty, she would reach back with her teeth, bite the saddle blanket and throw it on the ground. My grandfather knew immediately what was happening and started working with both of them. He used gentleness, kindness and patience to gain their trust. For a horse or dog to work with you as a partner, there has to be a bond of mutual trust and that you will take care of one another. With a little kindness, patience, work and time, they began to trust us, and became great horses that were gentle with children. It's amazing what a little kindness will do, but I would still wait for Rickey to exhale before I tightened the sinch. In the winter we would place a harness on beauty and tie one sled on behind the other. If we were too slow getting all the sleds tied together, she would turn her head around and look at us, as if to say "Aren't you people ready yet?" She was eager to get going. The person on the front sled held the reins and Beauty would pull us through the snow all over town. She started off in a walk. I believe she could hear us laughing and giggling, then she would break into a trot. It was great fun for all of us and I believe she enjoyed it also. When we were back at home, we would put Beauty in her stall, wipe her down and give her a favorite treat, carrots. Dolly on the other hand resisted all of our efforts. She would only allow our youngest sister to ride her. We boys were ejected into the air only to come crashing back down onto the hard ground to the amusement of my grandfather. We dare not say a bad word or get angry at her. There had to be a reason she was the way she was. We just hadn't figured it out yet. We later discovered she had a sore back and our sister was lighter weight than us boys. Rickey was eventually traded to a family with a young girl who loved him. My grandfather just couldn't resist a trade. It's like gambling, you never know for sure what you're going to get. Rickey got a great home with someone who loved him.

Every dog my grandfather ever had was named Sam except one. He was a raccoon dog named Spotty. He was white with black spots all over him, so not too difficult to come up with a name. Every fall my grandfather would receive calls from farmers where the raccoons were destroying their fields or contaminating their grain bins and ruining the grain. We would take Spotty and go to those farms raccoon hunting. Spotty would put his nose to the ground, find the scent and track the destructive raccoon down. My grandfather took me along as the pack mule. It was my job to carry the raccoons back to the car after he dispatched them. He sold the hides for whatever the going price was at the time. Sometimes it was $5 and in a good season up to $45. That was their Christmas money. Without it, Christmas was quite bleak. Nothing ever went to waste, the meat was donated to help others or we used it. I didn't care for it. It was very greasy and had a very wild taste and smell to it. When mixed into a stew with lots of potatoes, carrots, onions and corn, it was better, but not great. I knew what it was.

We raised almost all of our own food, chickens, ducks, geese, turkeys, and a huge garden. We would harvest the garden in the fall and my mother and grandmother would can everything for winter. There were three things I hated about raising our own food. Digging potatoes, cleaning out the dusty smelly chicken house and being chased by those nasty rotten geese. They followed us around everywhere just waiting for an opportunity to strike. When we weren't watching they would sneak up behind us, bite the back of our legs, then turn and run away. If anyone tripped and fell, the five geese would pile on top, biting us and beating us with their wings. The way you saved yourself was to grab the main goose on top of you by the neck to stop the biting, stand up, lift the goose by the neck into the air and then drop it onto the ground. They would then all run away flapping their wings wildly and honking, which sounded very much like laughing. One day the geese made a fatal mistake. It was fall and we were harvesting the garden. One of the little kids playing outside tripped and fell down. The geese piled on, biting at him and beating him with their wings. He was screaming loudly at being attacked. My grandfather was only a few steps away and in a matter of seconds there were no geese left alive. They had broken my grandfather's cardinal rule for animals. Thou shalt not harm a child. For that the geese paid the ultimate price. They had broken his rule and he had broken their necks. They would never bite anyone again. It was a harsh life that we lived, but again nothing ever went to waste. We had goose that year for Thanksgiving and Christmas dinner. My grandmother used the feathers to make a down comforter that kept her and my grandfather warm on cold winter nights.

It was now late summer. I was 10 years old and about to start 5th grade, Junior High. My mother, sister, brother and I had spent the day in Mason City buying school clothes and cloth material for dresses. Our mother could save money over the summer for this outing from not having to pay winter heating bills. We all looked forward to and would get excited about trying on new clothes that were crisp, colorful, unfaded, and no holes with patches. My brother and I got new clothes once a year at the beginning of school. They would be too big at the beginning with the hope that we would grow into them and not grow out of them before the end of the school year. We bought pants long enough so we could role the leg bottoms up into cuffs at the beginning of the school year and roll them down by the end as we grew. My mother was a wizard with a sewing machine and made my sister's clothes. They would excitedly shop and pour through patterns and bolts of cloth for what seemed like hours, while my brother and I would be bored to death. When we got home, they would with great care lay the cloth out on the dining room table, pin the patterns onto the cloth and cut out the designs. Then meticulously sew the pieces of cloth into wearable art. My sister would try them on, twirl around and then walk like a model to show them off. Girls were required to wear dresses or a skirt and a blouse to school. In the winter they were allowed to wear slacks beneath their dress or skirt to keep them warm while walking to and from school, but only if the temperature was below 10 degrees. They had to remove them immediately upon arrival at school and store them in their desk or locker. Boys had to wear a dress shirt, dress pants, or new jeans and a belt. No shorts, no T-shirts and no pictures or writing on your clothes was allowed. None of us were allowed, by our parents, to wear our new clothes before the first day of school, so we couldn't get them grass stained or worse, a hole.

After our trip to Mason City, I was thinking about the new clothes and how I wanted to make a good impression on the first day of school. It was important, because I was going into Junior High. I was no longer a child but also not an adult. I was an in-between. Being an in-between was very confusing. You are too old to do kid things or play with childish toys but too young for grownups. It was very awkward. You are not sure how you are supposed to act, so you do the only thing you know how to do best, and that is nothing. It's safer to do nothing than to take a chance and do something wrong or embarrassing. You are accused of being lazy, but what you are is confused and uncertain. My parents took care of that. They assigned me jobs, and I wasn't given a choice. The older I became, the more they expected me to be able to do. If I didn't know how to do something, they would teach me. I was not allowed to be confused or lazy. Even though no one ever said "good job" or "well done" and I grumbled about having to do the jobs. At the end of the day, I had a sense of belonging, of being needed, of being an integral part of something and had a feeling of accomplishment. I developed the self confidence that if a problem arose, I knew I could handle it. Donette's family did exactly the same thing.

That night in lying in bed, I was happy with the new clothes and with life. You know that little voice that we all have in our heads, the one some people call our conscience. The one that tells us when we've done something well or not so well. It suddenly and dramatically changed. It was now a crisp, clear and a booming voice inside my head. It was as if I heard it with my ears but it was inside my head. That startled me because it didn't feel like it came from me. There was no one upstairs in my room. Everyone was asleep in bed, but I heard, "You can live without love". Where did that come from? Why would I think that? The word love was never spoken in our house unless it was, I love ice cream, or I love cake. I don't remember anyone ever saying I love you. I don't remember my parents ever saying I love you to each other or to us as children. Looking back at this, why would a 10-year-old think such a thing? I didn't understand where this came from, but being 10, I didn't let it bother me and went to sleep.

The first time I actually remember meeting Donette was in Junior High, in 5th grade. We always had to sit in alphabetical order and the way the alphabet worked out, I sat on one side of her or the other depending on which side of the room they started seating. For some reason, I couldn't take my eyes off of her. She was so absolutely beautiful with long black hair that framed her face. When she looked my way, I would quickly look somewhere else to not look as though I was staring at her. I doubt she noticed me because she liked Lawrence, the cool good-looking kid who had the nicest clothes and played basketball, but he had eyes for someone else. For a small town in Iowa, she and I had unusual names, and we were both teased about our names. I think the other boys were trying to get her attention but were going about it in the wrong way. I didn't let it bother me but I could see it bothered her.

I would quietly say to her, "Don't let it bother you. They're just trying to get your attention." I could see that didn't help very much and it still bothered her deeply. "What's in a name? That which we call a rose by any other name would still smell as sweet." *-Romeo and Juliet-*

I was quite scared and shy whenever I talked to her. I said incredibly dumb sounding things trying to impress her and at the end of the day I would kick myself walking all the way home. In seventh grade, on the way to my next class, I saw her walking towards me talking with her friends. I wanted to avoid doing anything embarrassing so I quickly ducked out of sight into the nearest open door. I hadn't noticed, it was the girls' bathroom. The girls screamed. I leaped out of the door to land right in front of Donette. She saw me come out of the girls' bathroom. I was standing right in front of her. I was only inches away and couldn't be any closer. I said, "Ha, Ha, wrong door." She just smiled and shook her head yes. Meaning it certainly was the wrong door. I walked away shaking my head feeling extremely stupid, embarrassed and very angry at myself. It became painfully obvious that I was also not a great communicator. I didn't think I could kick myself hard enough on the way home for this one.

Donette was very kind to everyone. She always listened to me in class no matter how stupid I sounded, but the other kids let me know I lived on the south side of the railroad tracks. I was from the poor side of town, the Bloody Third Ward. I never found out why it was called that and I'm not sure anyone actually knew. Being from there and being teased about it definitely made me more determined to succeed. I would show them what success looks like. I decided that year that I would study science. Become a great scientist and be wealthy beyond my wildest dreams. I would show them. After all, Thomas Edison started out poor. "We know what we are, but know not, what we may be." *-William Shakespeare-*

In eighth grade, the gym teachers thought we should learn to dance. The instructors said dancing would be fun and great exercise, so they put the girls' and boys' gym classes together. The girls smiled and the boys moaned. The teachers chose the couples and put Donette and I together for height reasons we were told. We were going to learn to waltz. She took my hand, I put my other hand on her waist and she put her right hand on my shoulder. My "Tell Tale Heart" beat so hard and loud I was sure she must have heard it. At this age boys are not very coordinated and being nervous certainly didn't help. I at least didn't step on her feet, but I was less than impressive. Rhythm was not something I had been granted and I so wanted to impress her. She wanted to dance with handsome Lawrence.

That fall, my cousin Laurie had a boy and girl Halloween party. She cut cardboard pumpkins into two pieces with irregular shapes, half went into a box the girls drew out of and the other half into a box for the boys. It was purely a random chance which partner you had for the party. Donette's half matched mine. They fit together perfectly. My heart pounded out of my chest and my mouth was dry. I tried to talk about things I thought she would like, but I said things that were incredibly stupid and I could tell she was not impressed. She didn't say anything but left the party early. After the party I kicked myself all the way home. I was very angry at myself for being so stupid and now felt that I would never be good enough for her.

In 1959 Nikita Khrushchev, the premier of Russia, stood at the podium of the United Nations, took his shoe off, beat it on the podium and said "We will bury you". It was televised in fuzzy black and white and after he said that, no one heard anything else he said. That was enough and the cold war was on. People started building fallout shelters in their basements and underground in their backyards. There were fallout shelters built by towns with signs posted everywhere directing you to their location. Civil Defense Sirens were installed. There were public service announcements on TV and at the movie theater about how to protect yourself and your family. The fear of possible nuclear war was being instilled in everyone's mind by newspapers, magazines, radio and TV news programs. The Osage school system started doing nuclear bomb drills called "Duck and Cover drills." They would ring the class dismiss bell rapidly. We were to quickly duck under our desks kneeling face down then cover our face and head with our hands and arms. These drills at school went on for only a short time. Just how long I don't remember. The drills started off monthly, then gradually disappeared and no one missed them. I remember one drill in Junior High where the bell rang and our teacher Mrs. Pitts yelled "Duck and Cover!" Kids dove under their desks except for me. I was sick of these drills as was everyone else. I said, "I'm sorry Mrs. Pitts but I forgot my duck, may I please go home and cover him?" I received a look from Mrs. Pitts that was reminiscent of the look on the Wicked Witch of the Wests face when she discovered Dorothy had dropped a house on her sister. With her scrawny crooked index finger, she pointed at my desk. I sheepishly crawled under my desk, face down and covered my head. I thought that I was mumbling to myself, under my hands and arms, but it actually turned out to be out loud. I said, "Do they really think Russia is going to bomb Osage Iowa? The only thing they will hit here is some cows, a few pigs and a lot of corn. We are out in the middle of nowhere. If they did bomb us, does the school really think these desks will protect us?" I then heard a muffled giggle to my right. I moved my right arm just enough to see Donette looking at me and smiling. Maybe what I had been mumbling about made sense and reassured her, or maybe I had been myself and not trying to impress anyone.

After eighth grade graduation, my father thought I was old enough to get a summer job. I thought I had enough work to do around home with the animals and garden. I went to work at the gas station that he managed. He taught me how to pump gas, service cars, fix tires, change brakes, replace exhaust systems and much more. He never yelled at me. He would just say,"Here, let me show you how to do that." He gave me my work ethic, taught me to be meticulous in my work and how to be safe. Most important of all, he taught me how to relate to people. How to tell if someone was having a good day or not. When to speak or when to be quiet and listen. Not just hear but to actively listen. There is a difference. All of this was learning how to pay attention. I didn't know it at the time how extremely important this skill would become in later years and how the lack of it would affect my life.

On the other hand, there was my mother. Five feet six inches in height and packed full of pure dynamite. She was ahead of her time. She had developed into a strong willed, honest person who had her own opinions and spoke her mind. If she thought it, she said it, no matter what or who she was talking to or about. Half of the town was afraid of her but not the children. She had a soft spot in her heart for them. She drove school bus on and off for almost 43 years. Some of the school bus drivers didn't like the kids, but not her. At Christmas she would need help with all the presents from her bus kids, and that was how she referred to them as "my bus kids." We would be walking down Main Street and the adults coming toward us, would see her then suddenly start to cross over to the other side of the street. The kids who were with them would try to pull away from their parents to talk to her but were dragged along to the other side. It was a very obvious avoidance and I thought it was humorous.

My mother and father were getting ready to go dancing one Saturday evening. She looked very nice. She had on makeup, ear rings and a very pretty red dress. She was looking at herself in the tall mirror on the closet door, complaining about being too thin and flat chested. She said, "It's you kid's fault, you drank me dry." We knew she didn't mean what she said, or at least I hoped she didn't mean it. I thought she was just joking, but then a few days later she purchased that infamous T-shirt. It was a yellow T-shirt that had two white fried eggs with yellow yolks strategically placed side by side on the front of the shirt. This was the early 60s. You weren't allowed to say toilet paper in public. Husbands and wives on television were not allowed to be seen in the same bed. Pregnant teachers had to retire before they started showing and corrupted their students. The T-shirt became the talk of the town. If people had to talk to her, they would stare at their feet or look off into space trying not to look at the shirt. People in stores would do rock paper scissors or flip a coin to see who had to wait on her. I was so thankful that I had to go to work instead of shopping. My brother and sister were not as fortunate. We thought this was revenge on us for all the embarrassing things we did as children. Like my trip to the doctor and my brother, when he was three, lifting up the back of her dress over his head at a wedding.

In High School, I continued to work in the gas station with my father after school and on weekends. Donette did baby sitting and worked part time as a waitress. I would go to that restaurant whenever I could and order a shake or sundae to see if she was working. There was just something very special about her that gave me a feeling I just couldn't explain and I couldn't get her out of my mind. She was always there, always on my mind. I got my driver's license four months before Donette. One evening I was driving home from work and I saw a lovely young woman in a sleek 1957 yellow Plymouth convertible with the top down, having trouble. She had a scarf tied over head to protect her hair from the wind. A white blouse and tan form fitting jeans. It was an absolute gorgeous scene out of a movie with her standing next to the car. It was Donette. I stopped and asked if she would like a ride. She said, "I would, thank you." I had known her almost all of my life, so on the way to her father's shop for help, I dredged up enough courage to ask her, "If you're not doing anything on Friday night. Would you like to go to the drive-in theater with me?" I held my breath in anticipation and prepared myself for the worst, until she said, "That sounds like fun. I would like that." I picked her up on a warm Friday evening. I tried to just be myself and I managed to not say anything dumb that entire night. We laughed and enjoyed each other's company immensely. When I took her home, I drove under the speed limit to make the evening last as long as I could. It was wonderful. When we finally arrived at her home, I walked her to the door and said, "I had a great time tonight." She said, "I did too." I asked, "What are you doing tomorrow?" She answered, "Nothing." I asked," Would you like to do nothing together?" She answered, "I would like that." She gave me a kiss on the cheek and said goodnight. That was the beginning of our life. We have been together ever since.

Donette and I would meet in the hall between classes just to see each other. I could barely stand to be away from her. If we didn't have class together, I would walk her to her next class then walk as fast as I could to mine so as not to be late. Donette and I would hold hands when I walked her to her next class. Miss Patterson, the old sour puss business and typing teacher that didn't like me very much. Would see us holding hands. Then she would rush at us like a charging bull with her hands outstretched in front of her, put her hands between us and push us apart. "No holding hands in school" we were told by Miss Patterson who also said, "You know what that leads to." I answered, "No, what?" There was that wicked witch of the west scowl again. She liked Donette and even recommended her for a job at a local bank, but now she really didn't care much for me. At the end of the school day, I would take Donette to her home hoping for a kiss goodby before I went to work.

After High School graduation, I continued to work in the Osage gas station pumping gas and fixing cars while attending junior college 30 miles away in Mason City. Donette worked as a book keeper in the local bank. We spent every spare minute we could together. It was 1968 and we were 19. On a very nice sunny spring Saturday afternoon we decided to go to a movie matinee in Mason City Iowa. It was Romeo and Juliet. It was done in Shakespear's original dialogue, except for the music. There was a particular song that struck a chord with both of us and I couldn't get it out of my mind, entitled "A Time for Us." I eventually learned all the words to that song and would unconsciously start to sing it, but only when I was alone. (Remember this song.)

After we left the movie theater, we were walking slowly down Federal Avenue to my car. I believe we were discussing how we didn't care for the unhappy ending. Who would write a story where the lovers both died? I turned to speak to Donette and she wasn't there. She was behind me looking in a store display window. I asked her what she was doing, she answered with a smile and said, "Just looking. Can we go in and just look around?" I said, "Of course." It was a jewelry store. When we were 17, she had saved her waitress tips and bought me a gold ring with a beautiful red garnet stone in the center from our local jewelry store. I wore it constantly. Donette loved jewelry. She loved ear rings, necklaces and bracelets. Anything that sparkled. The clerk came over and asked if he could help her and she replied, "I'm just looking." He smiled and pulled out a tray of rings and handed her one to try on. She didn't care for that one. He handed her another. It was a gold band with a single small raised diamond in the center. She put it on the ring finger of her left hand and started to smile with that look I just couldn't resist. I loved her with all my heart and that was the very first time it really struck me what I had been feeling. I was deeply in love with her. I said, "If you really like that one, I think you should keep it." I look back on that as one of the best days of my life, and I remember it as if it was yesterday.

In Iowa, in 1968, girls could get married at age 16 without their parents' permission. I thought that was strange because boys had to be 21. We were both 19. So eloping was out of the question because of my age. My parents had to go with me, in person, to the courthouse and sign papers giving me permission to get married. How embarrassing, but I didn't care. I would have done anything. I loved her with all my heart. So, two 19-year-old kids who didn't have a clue as to what the future may hold and we had almost no money between us. But we loved each other with all of our hearts, were married that same summer on August 25th 1968. It was a small wedding at a very lovely little church that Donette attended with her family and where she taught Sunday school to children. When I saw her, in her wedding gown, walking down the aisle beside her father I couldn't stop smiling. She was so incredibly beautiful. All I knew was that I loved her with all my heart and that day, I was the luckiest person on earth to be chosen by her. "I do love nothing in the world, so well as you." *-William Shakespeare-*

Two days after the wedding, my mother was walking out of the bank on Main Street when she was stopped by one of the town gossips and busybodies. All little towns have them and Osage certainly had its quota. She told my mother she had seen the wedding announcement in the newspaper and proceeded to ask, "When is the baby due?" After all, why would two 19-year old's get married. With my mother's history and how I was born. That was the wrong question to ask.

The person who told me the story was on main street that day. She doubted Mrs. Busybody would be on the same side of the street as my mother ever again. This very loud explosive exchange mainly on my mother's part got the attention of everyone on main street that day. My mother backed Mrs. Busybody up so far, she almost fell backwards off the curb into the street. The person who told me the story was concerned that Mrs. Busybody may have had a wound on her chest from my mother's index finger. She was uniquely informed that Donette was not pregnant and there was no baby. This confrontation between a town gossip and my mother somewhat improved my mother's standing in the hearts of some members of the community. But now, not surprisingly enough, even more people that happened to be walking on Main Street that day found the other side of the street to be more appealing and would suddenly cross the street to the other side. We now know why the chickens crossed the road. They were afraid of my mother.

After we were married, Donette and I moved to Mason City where I started school at North Iowa Area Community College. I went part time at night and had fulltime work at Frozen Foods Inc as a delivery driver during the day. I made $100 dollars per week and took home $80. Donette worked part time at Arlen's clothing store for $2 an hour. We had a 1962 Plymouth Valiant that whenever we hit a pot hole or railroad tracks at night the head lights would suddenly go out. If I got out of the car, opened the hood and slammed it shut several times very hard the lights would return. One person stopped, rolled down his window and wanted to know why I was so angry at the car. I said I wasn't angry. I was just turning on the headlights. He got a strange look on his face, rolled up his window and left before I had a chance to explain that it had a short in the wiring somewhere and I couldn't find it. One day, while I was concentrating on trying to find that short in the wiring and not paying close attention to Donette, she said, "Wouldn't it be nice if we had a baby?" I thought to myself, yes it would be nice to have a baby in the future when I'm out of school, have a good job and things are stable, but I actually said, while concentrating on what I was trying to find, "That would be nice." Women are very good at multitasking. Men, not so much.

A few months later, Donette and I went out for a special evening. She became ill after eating spaghetti at a local restaurant called Oscars. On the drive home, I had to pull the car over to a complete stop, where she opened the door and started throwing up. I was worried and I blamed it on the spaghetti. I thought she had food poisoning. We were never going to eat at that horrible restaurant again. The food poisoning didn't go away, she was nauseated and threw up the next day so we went to the doctor. When she came out of the doctor's office with the biggest Cheshire Cat smile on her face and walked briskly with a bounce in her step towards me. I was confused. I found out, Donette had stopped taking her birth control pills. I said, "I thought we were going to discuss this before we decided." She answered, "We did." I had to sit down. If this was a 1950s movie, she would have said, "The rabbit died." Donette was elated, and we could eat at Oscar's again.

In the spring of 1970, our son was born in the Osage hospital. Donette had kept her family doctor even though we lived in Mason City. There was no ultrasound in those days but Donette knew somehow that we were going to have a son. Fathers were not allowed in the delivery room, and families were not even allowed to visit. Family members had to stand outside on the lawn and look through a window to see the baby in the nursery. I was at least allowed in Donette's hospital room. Her nurse handed me a pencil and pad of paper then said," I need you to time her contractions." I did it diligently, succinctly and exactly right down to the second. I felt like I was participating instead of just being an observer. It must be important or she wouldn't have asked me to do it. So, I meticulously filled page after page with exact times of when the contractions started and how long each and every contraction lasted. It was a masterpiece of organization and information. When it came time for Donette to deliver and they were there to get her. I tried to give them the important pad filled with exact times, but no one knew what I was talking about. They told me to wait in the waiting room. I was dumb founded and confused. I walked slowly down to the waiting room clutching the pad and pencil in my tight grip, clenching my jaw with the knowledge and realization that I had not been participating in the birth and that I had been duped. That sneaky conniving nurse had used that pad and pencil to keep me occupied and out of her way. It had worked very successfully. I felt rather foolish and upset at being duped at such an important time. There is nothing more important in our lives than the birth of our children. I had concentrated on what I was doing so hard, because I believed it to be important for Donette, that it kept me separated from her. I had been lied to by a person in whom I trusted. That trust had now been damaged and it would leave a lasting impression on me. I would be very skeptical of anything I was told in the future no matter who it came from.

It was late afternoon and I was the only person in the waiting room. The magazines were old and out dated. Some even had pages that were so old they had turned yellow. I looked around and noticed the "no smoking" sign on the bulletin board, but the ashtrays were still there just in case. There were burn marks on the arms of some of the chairs where fathers had laid their cigarettes down and forgot them when they rushed off to see their newborn. I was still quite upset about being so foolish that I didn't feel like sitting down. I had already been sitting for hours taking exact times and writing them down. I walked around the room feeling useless. It made me upset enough that I broke the pencil in half, threw it and the pad of exact times into the trash. I took some deep breathes and tried to calm down. It was over and done. It served no purpose being upset. It could only make things worse and I wanted to be comforting for Donette who I knew was going to be exhausted but very happy.

It didn't take long until I heard a baby cry, then the sneaky nurse came to get me and show me our son. He was all pink and wonderful. The feeling of foolishness and being upset that I had, completely disappeared. It was replaced by a feeling of pride and love. I got a strange feeling in my chest as it seemed to warm my heart. He certainly had a good set of lungs, screaming out loud at the top of his voice after being so rudely forced into this world. Donette had made me promise I would count all of his fingers and toes because I had a relative with an extra thumb and an aunt with webbed toes who was an excellent swimmer. When I was able to see Donette again, that was the first thing she asked and was relieved by the answer. I was so proud of her. We had no health insurance and the total delivery bill came to an immense sum of money for us, $400. That was five weeks of my take home income and we were just barely getting by with two of us working. Donette did not work now with a baby at home. I have never seen her happier. Work was kind and gave me a 10 per cent raise to $110 dollars a week and I took home $90. We made monthly payments on the hospital bill and at Christmas we made the final payment. That was our only Christmas gift to each other that year. We officially owned our son. We felt like the young couple in O. Henry's short story "The Gift of the Magi" as to what was actually important. We had very little but we loved each other with all of our hearts and I was so proud of our family.

It's now fall 1972 and our son Robert is 2 years old. I transferred to the University of Iowa and we moved to Iowa City. The home of the Iowa Hawkeyes football team. For $120 a month, we had a small one-bedroom end apartment on the ground floor of a two-story complex at Town and Campus apartments. Above us lived a young couple with a 2-year-old son. The apartment beside us had a young single mom with a 7-year-old daughter. Above them were two college boys sharing the apartment. The complex was made up of several four plex buildings connected by sidewalks, staircases and balconies. It was a quiet place except for the occasional pleasant sounds of children playing outside. Early one Saturday morning Donette and I heard a loud blood curdling scream from next door. I raced out of our front door to find the single mom standing on the sidewalk clutching her daughter tightly. Both of them with bare feet and still in their pajamas.

They were staring at their open front door. She looked at me, pointed at the door and said with a shaky voice "Snake!" I moved closer, peered through the open door and could see into the brightly lit bathroom where there appeared to be a snake coiled in the far corner. I hate snakes. If it had been anything else, I would have gone in there, but a snake? I was not going in there. The two college boys from upstairs must have heard the loud scream and came flying out of their door. They raced down the stairs, through the open apartment door and into the bathroom as if they were specifically looking for something. When they emerged, one of them had the four-foot snake draped over his shoulders and said "It's just our pet corn snake Ralph. He's harmless." Both of them then quickly disappeared upstairs into their apartment. The only way this could have happened would be if the snake slithered its way into the open toilet above, crawled straight down the sewer pipe and out the toilet below. This is the stuff of horror movies and nightmares. It could lead to a permanent lifelong fear of snakes in the toilet. Ophidiophobia. The single mom went immediately to the complex manager and the two boys and snake ultimately disappeared. In our apartment, reading time in the bathroom disappeared. The age-old male and female debate over the toilet seat being left up or down had been resolved for everyone in the lower apartments of the complex by a single event. Our seat was down and the lid was always closed. It remains that way to this day.

Donette was working hard with two jobs to support us. She went to work in the morning as a receptionist in the lab at the University hospital. Worked all day and then went to her second part time job after supper at Sears in the credit department. I went to school, took care of our son, our apartment and did odd jobs for money whenever I could. Robert and I went everywhere together either by city bus or riding on my bicycle. City bus was 25 cents. Gas for the car was expensive, 50 cents a gallon so we didn't drive very often. There were times when we only had macaroni and cheese, peanut butter and a few cans of soup for the entire week, but no one complained. I felt guilty about Donette working so hard. She never said anything but I could see she was getting tired. I decided to apply and was accepted into the University of Iowa College of Medicine's brand-new Physician's Assistant program. I gave up the idea of trying for medical school like I had planned. This would allow me to graduate sooner and start working to support my family. My father had given up his dream for his family. I could do no less. I loved them with all my Heart.

The University of Iowa College of Medicine had a huge anatomy laboratory. The first day of class all 20 of us in the PA program walked into the lab together with all the other medical students. Seeing all of the individual bodies wrapped in clear plastic on tables lined up clear across this immense room was a bit overwhelming. The sight of the bodies and the smell of formaldehyde used to preserve them was too much for some of the students. For many this was the first time for seeing a dead body. No one close to them had yet passed away. A few had to step out of the lab, take some deep breaths, gather themselves together and come back in. The bodies all had death certificates with a picture of the person attached to it. Some of us wandered around reading the death certificates out of morbid curiosity as to how they ended up here in the anatomy laboratory. The majority were donated to science by the person themselves. A few were named John or Jane Doe. These were unclaimed unidentified bodies that were donated by cities to save money on funeral costs. Thank Heavens it's not Europe in medieval times. Where we would have to watch the cemeteries for a fresh burial, sneak into the cemetery on a moonless night, dig up the body, whisk it away to a secret laboratory to study anatomy with the risk of possible arrest. Leonardo da Vinci would hire grave robbers to dig up bodies so he could study anatomy prior to making his most famous works of art.

One of our students recognized a name on one of the death certificates and the girl's picture. It was a young pretty nurse that he knew and worked with at a hospital in Des Moines, Iowa. He remembered that she had committed suicide with pills and alcohol. Some of us thought that was rather specific knowledge. He stood solemnly there staring at her picture for several moments. The look on his face had a few of us believing there was more to the story than we knew. What were the odds of both of them being in the same place at the same time? In a medical school laboratory, one as a subject and one as a student. They were over 100 miles away from where they knew each other. If this was a coincidence and truly a random occurrence. It was absolutely phenomenal and unbelievable. He requested to be assigned to a table as far away from her dissection table as possible. That request was granted.

At the beginning, dissecting a human body just didn't feel right to any of us. We all felt we were violating this body that once was a living, breathing, walking, talking, human being. A real person with a life and possibly a family. Some of us questioned it, because it just didn't feel like a fitting end to someone's only life. We were told by our instructors that these people were voluntarily here to grant us the gift of knowledge to be able to help others. That thought did help a great deal. In time the work and studying became routine. As human beings, we can adapt and become accustomed to almost anything. A few people brought in lunches, snacks and other goodies to eat while working and studying. I could not do it. It became exciting when the first person found the cause of death listed on the death certificate was wrong, and from then on what we were doing became a forensic investigation in our own minds. We found cancers that were unknown. A woman with 7 kidneys that all appeared to have been functioning. One of the John Does was listed as having died of a heart attack, in which we found a bullet. Maybe he died of a heart attack because of the pure mental shock of someone shooting him.

At lunch we would all sit at the big round table in the cafeteria and discuss what we were doing and what we had found. We all reeked of formaldehyde. It permeated our clothing and the people who could hear us and smell us at surrounding tables would get grossed out then go elsewhere to eat. Riding home on the bus, no one would sit near to me. If I was the only person waiting at the bus stop, the bus would drive right past without even slowing down and I would hear the faint cheers from the people inside the bus as it passed by. At home, Donette would make me take my clothes off at the front door and take a shower with heavily scented shampoo and soap before she or Robert would come near me. Despite all of this I enjoyed learning anatomy.

In the spring semester there was a class called living anatomy. It was the beginning of being taught how to do physical examinations. It was routine to split the class into male and female classes because you learned physical examination by examining each other. This semester they didn't have enough instructors to do the split classes. Our instructor asked us, if it would be alright, if they kept us co-ed. Being sophisticated educated adults, we all raised our hands and said, "Sure." He said, "Great, we'll plan on that." Then he told us, that for the first class being held in two days, we would have to strip down to our underwear or less and then he left. We were stunned. We all felt like that should have been crucial information that was known before we voted. That night at supper I explained this to Donette who did not take the information well. I explained to her that I didn't like this either. She said, "They can't do this, you're not going!" I said, "I have to go. If I don't pass this course then everything we've done, everything we've sacrificed for and struggled through in the past few years is for nothing." We finished supper without speaking further. She got up and said, "I'll be back," and left. Robert went to play with his toys, I cleared the table and washed the dishes. I was worried about Donette. She didn't have to work that evening and had driven off in the car. She was gone for some time and I became quite concerned about her. Later in the evening, when she returned, she handed me a package. She had spent what little money she had on new men's undershirts and shorts. I took her in my arms and said, "It's going to be OK." She jokingly said a line from an old I Love Lucy, "Be careful of those wicked city women."

Just after New Year's Day of 1975, I was on my surgery rotation dressed in green scrubs, a white coat, a stethoscope in my pocket and on my way to lunch. At the University of Iowa Hospital cafeteria there were two lines. One for employees and students where you pay for your meals. One for doctors where it's free. I had no money. I slipped quietly and nonchalantly into the back of the doctor's line hoping not to be noticed. At the front of the line, with his tray of food in hand, was one of the older white haired very well-liked doctors who taught medical students. He suddenly dropped his tray, clutched his chest and fell to the floor. The other doctors in line dropped their trays and immediately started CPR, rushed in a crash cart, shocked him and remarkably got him back. He was not very happy to be back. He asked them what was wrong with them? Why couldn't they hear him? He was standing right over there, pointing to a corner of the room. He said, He was trying to communicate to them that he was alright and to leave him alone. We all thought he had hallucinated. After the commotion was all over, and they had taken him to the intensive care unit. One of the doctors pointed out that he had collapsed before he even tasted the hospital's food. I got lunch and thought it was good. It was free.

In the spring and summer, I did a few medical rotations at Broadlawns Polk County hospital in Des Moines, Iowa. I did my Intensive care, pediatrics and ER rotations there. They had dorm rooms for the students to stay in while we were away from home. The hospital was located in a very rough Des Moines neighborhood. One of my classmates, who was an avid runner, would get up early every morning to go running and run on the streets surrounding the hospital. People that lived there would throw rocks and sticks at him. They would sick their dogs on him, and he would be stopped by the police, handcuffed, frisked and then released. He was told by nurses at the hospital, "The only people that run in this neighborhood have committed a crime or have stolen something." They all thought he was crazy for running in the neighborhood. That he would be mugged, injured and end up as a patient in the ER or worse. He stubbornly persisted, would smile, wave and say good morning as he ran by the hospital's neighbors. He became a regular running in the neighborhood every day. People stopped throwing sticks and stones and would wave back. He was no longer chased by dogs and the police would wave as they drove by. Everyone was amazed. He had elevated people's spirits with just a smile, a wave and persistence. A slight bit of normality had returned to the neighborhood.

Broadlawns was a very interesting place to learn. It had some of the most dedicated hard-working people I've ever worked with and some not. No one was there expecting to get rich. Most were there from a desire and a purpose. It was difficult work both emotionally and physically. They saw the worst things that life had to offer. At the end of their shift, they were exhausted. It was a different type of exhaustion. It was the type of exhaustion that made you get up and do it again the next day. You had made a difference. I saw everything there. Knifings, gunshot wounds, horrific vehicle accidents, child abuse, drug over doses. I removed all kinds of battery powered things from places they should never have been. I had knives pulled on me. One of the residents had a gun pulled on him and dove head first over the admissions desk as our police officer in the ER wrestled the person to the floor. One evening a large black sedan with blacked out windows roared past the ER entrance. Without slowing down, the back door opened and a body was thrown from the car. It rolled down the street and came to rest face down against the curb. A valiant effort was made to save him but he had way too many injuries. Multiple broken bones, internal hemorrhage and head trauma. Not all of which were from being thrown from the car. He died in the ICU two days later. The Sheriff's department identified him and found out he was on the FBIs ten most wanted list for grand theft auto. We surmised that he must have stolen the wrong persons car.

There was the cutest little elderly Haitian lady who came into the ER frequently. We all loved listening to her. She had the most marvelous Caribbean accent. She would come in almost weekly complaining about pain in her feet. She made all of us feel uncomfortable watching her walk. She looked in pain as if she was walking barefoot on broken glass. Her feet were swollen, pale in color and looked painful. The problem had been completely worked up by several specialists and was determined to be from a lack of circulation. Arteries that could not carry enough blood because they had simply become too small and narrow. There was nothing more that could be done. She had already tried every prescribed and herbal remedy she could find but nothing helped. Each time she came into the ER she was seen by the same supervising physician. She liked him because he was so kind to her. This day he grabbed me and three residents. Pulled us into the large trauma room. Set our little lady on the exam table in the middle of the room. Asked if anyone could play drums. One of the residents said he did. The supervisor handed the bewildered resident a large metal basin upside down and said, "Give me your best Bongo beat." He then turned out the lights. Aimed the overhead lamp onto her feet, picked up a box of talcum powder and began to chant. The resident sat down and the bongo beat started. Our supervisor started twirling, dancing and chanting around the exam table. Each time he passed by her feet he would sprinkle powder on them. The other two residents picked up boxes of powder and joined in the dance and chant. The chant sounded somewhere between Gregorian and Native American. It made no sense what so ever. I slid quietly back into a dark corner. I was trying to be as small and inconspicuous as possible. What on earth had I gotten myself into. I was a student with trust issues trying to distance myself from this craziness and I had no idea what was going on. The bongo beat, dancing and chanting became faster and faster, louder and louder until it culminated with all three of them standing in front of her. The supervisor raised his arms over his head and shouted at her feet, "Evil spirits be gone." Everything became quiet. He smiled at her and said, "How do you feel dear?" She said, "I think I feel better." She put on her shoes, thanked everyone and walked almost normally out the door. I thought about this for a little while. There was no scientific medical reason this should have worked. If it did help, it had to be mind over matter. I had seen videos of people having surgery under just hypnosis. One woman was wide awake while she had part of her lung removed. The mind can be a powerful tool when you have faith and believe. The supervisor looked at me and said, "You should have joined in," I needed an excuse and replied, "I don't have rhythm." I didn't see her again before the end of my ER rotation. I often wondered how she was doing, and if it was still working. "There are more things in heaven and earth, Horatio, than are dreamt of in your philosophy." *-Hamlet-*.

My required psychiatric rotation was at Mount Pleasant Mental Hospital in Mount Pleasant Iowa. It was a particularly snowy winter that year and Donette and Robert were over 4 hours' drive away when it was good weather. I was not looking forward to this rotation, because I would be away from Donette for six weeks. I was only able to go home every other weekend if the weather was good, which it frequently wasn't. It was a very old hospital built out of stone and brick. It could have easily been the setting for the movie, "One Flew Over the Cuckoo's Nest." It housed the worst of the worst.

When I arrived, I was given a small dorm room that had a single bed, tiny refrigerator and a desk with a gooseneck lamp. I believe these rooms were the old unused Nun's quarters when Nuns took care of patients in the hospital. My first day there, I was assigned to a social worker who was obviously not happy with having a new student assigned to her. From another room through a window, I could see her drop her shoulders, roll her eyes and she shook her head at being told the news. She glanced at me in the other room and reluctantly motioned with her hand for me to accompany her. As we walked, she started asking questions. She asked if I was married and had children. I answered, "Yes, and I have a son." She wanted to know my birthday and Donette's birthday. She suddenly stopped walking, turned to me and flipantly said, "Oh, Scorpio and Pisces. You're not compatible. You will never make it together." She turned and started walking again. That took me by surprise. She callously uttered that statement as if it was a universal truth and a matter of fact. She didn't know us. I had only met her just ten minutes ago and now she flippantly says we will never make it. I love Donette with all my heart.

She ushered me into a small room, sat me down and put a booklet on the table in front of me. Then said, "This is the MMPI test that we give all the new patients. When you are finished, bring it out and I will score it for you." Then she left the room and closed the door. I heard her say to a co-worker, "That will keep him occupied for a while." MMPI stands for Minnesota Multiphasic Personality Inventory. Its 338 questions with multiple choice answers. I was still not happy about the "You will never make it" statement, but as a student, I didn't say anything. I felt as though my family had been attacked, and all of the protective defense mechanisms of a man in love with his family welled up inside of me. This was my family and I loved them with all my heart. Love is emotional and is never logical. I opened the test booklet and started reading the test as she requested. The questions were simple questions and you chose the multiple-choice answer that you felt best fits you. Very quickly, I realized that it asked the same question four different times in four different ways. The idea behind this, is that a so-called normal person will answer the questions the same each time. If the question is, what is your favorite color and your favorite color is blue, you will answer blue each time the question is asked differently. Depending on how you answer the questions determines the scope of your personality. A thought crossed my mind and it was not a logical thought. It was a defiantly emotional thought. A thought that made a smile or better yet, a smirk appear upon my face. A diabolical plan had just been hatched. I made sure that I answered each of the four versions of each question differently. When completed, I went to her desk and calmly handed the test papers to her. She gave a sigh of inconvenience, opened a drawer, pulled out a template and laid it over the answer sheet. If you don't read the questions in a multiple-choice test and just randomly mark answers, without reading them, statistically you will still get some answers that match. I was sure that she would notice this and realize that I had purposely sabotaged the test and we could discuss her flippant comment, but she didn't notice. Her eyes suddenly became very large, she turned pale as if every drop of blood had suddenly drained from her face. She shoved the test and template across the desk over to where I stood, then said, "Here, you score it yourself." She very quickly stood up and briskly walked out of the room as if she was late for an appointment. I did as she asked, I used the template and scored the test, even though I knew it was going to be false. Let me, if I may, translate what it said from psychiatric speak into layman's terms. It essentially read, "Homicidal Sex Maniac." Well, this didn't turn out quite as I had expected. I gave a muffled nervous laugh that was heard by other staff in the room. I mistakenly left the test on her desk and exited through an open door. I went back to my dorm room, sat down on the bed and remorse started to set in. What I did with that test may have been one of the dumbest things I have ever done.

The next day upon arising, I received a hand written message quietly slipped under the door of my dorm room. It said to report to the psychiatrist at the locked male ward as his new student. When I reported to the psychiatrist that morning, I was greeted by a psychiatrist with a very strange look on his face. He said, "You're my new student?" I said, "That's what they told me." He replied, "Have you had psychiatric training in the past because I usually get residents. They never send me new students. Why would they send a new student to the most dangerous lock-up ward in the hospital?" I asked if I may sit down and he motioned with his hand to take a seat. I explained the "You will never make it" statement from the social worker that caused every protective instinct in my body to well up and what I did with the MMPI test as a result. I told him about the hand written note slipped under my dorm room door and I handed it to him. Then I said, "This morning, on my way here, people coming toward me in the hallway all moved over against the wall and stared at me as I went by. I ducked into the restroom to look at my clothing and to make sure my fly wasn't open. It wasn't. When the Catholic chaplain got off the elevator that I was waiting for, he gave me the sign of the cross and uttered something in Latin as he moved sideways away from me along the wall. I smiled and thanked him. For what, I don't know." As I sat there, across the desk from the psychiatrist, feeling rather foolish about what I had done and fearful that I may be kicked out of school. I could see a smile slowly appearing on the psychiatrist's face. He leaned back in his overstuffed leather desk chair, crossed his arms in front of him, looked up at the ceiling and began to roar with laughter as he realized why I had been sent to him. He laughed so loud, his secretary came into the room and asked, "Is everything alright?" Still laughing the psychiatrist said, "Mary, this is our new student for the next six weeks, would you introduce him to the staff and make sure he has what he needs." She looked at me with a strange look on her face and said, "New student?" He clasped his hands together in front of him, turned to me and said, "We are going to do just fine. It's a pleasure to meet you. How long do you think we should wait before we tell them what you did?" I replied, "I don't care if we ever tell them." He replied, "No, no we need to tell them. I think a week will be just right. It will take them at least that long to organize their pitchforks and torches." I said, "Pitchforks and torches?" He replied, "That's a metaphor. I'm definitely looking forward to this Friday's staff meeting." As Mary took me to meet the other staff on the ward, we could hear him still laughing. She said, "Whatever you did sure made his day."

The next six weeks were very interesting. The first patient group session, that I was allowed to sit in on, led by the Psychiatrist, was very surprising. There were five male patients, the Psychiatrist and myself sitting in a wide circle on folding metal chairs that had seen better days. There were three big, burly, muscular orderlies standing strategically outside of the circle. There was one particular patient out of the five, that was sitting straight across from me, that sat there with his arms crossed staring at the the floor and refusing to speak. About midway through the session he started raising his eyes and staring forward, then raised his head looking straight at me. He suddenly jumped up, pointed at me with his outstretched arm and index finger. Then shouted, "You, you killed my wife!" Instantly the orderlies sprang into action. One held him back and the other two each grabbed one of my arms, lifted me up, out and over the chair, then out the door we went with the door locked behind us. I yelled, "Wait, what did I do!" One of the orderlies said, "You didn't do anything. That patient was in prison for two years and when he got out, he found that his wife was pregnant. He became so enraged and angry, he took a butcher knife from the kitchen and cut the baby out her, killing both of them. After he realized what he had done, he had a mental breakdown and ended up in here. He still can't accept what he has done and will randomly pick someone out, accuse them of killing his wife and try to strangle them. You can't be around him again." I very humbly thanked the orderlies and from then on, I only sat in on the juvenile sessions.

After the Friday staff meeting, which I was not allowed to attend, people stopped hugging the walls in the hallways and said good morning with a smile. Security guards would laugh and give me the thumbs up sign. The Catholic chaplain still gave me the sign of the cross and said, "Bless you, my son." I said, "You know father, I'm not Catholic." He said, "It doesn't matter. God works in mysterious ways," and he walked away chuckling. I didn't see the social worker again, but I was told she was still around. I learned a great deal about people in those six weeks and what a fine line there was between sanity and insanity along with how little it takes for some sane people to lose it. Also, how quickly a rumor can spread and be believed. I now realize how very fortunate that I didn't end up on the ward as a patient or kicked out of school. At the end of the six weeks, the psychiatrist wanted to know what I thought about my experience with the patients and did I learn anything useful. I responded in glowing terms as befitting a student who wanted a good grade, but I had learned a great deal. Then he said, "What do you think about the people we have that hear voices. What if it's not all in their head and some actually hear voices? We know so little about how the brain actually functions." He smiled then said, "Never mind. Have a safe trip home and a wonderful Christmas. It's been a pleasure having you here and I am definitely going to use the MMPI story in my lectures." I drove through a blizzard that night and was immensely glad and thankful to be home with Donette and Robert that Christmas. Even though we didn't have much, we had each other. Love is a very powerful emotion and is not logical. It can result in immense joy, immense pain and yes, a little stupidity. I love my family with all my heart.

I'm on the first day of my second general surgery rotation that summer, but the first one at the VA hospital. I haven't yet officially met the surgeon to who's teaching service I had been assigned. This was not the first time at this hospital. I had gone through an internal medicine rotation there and I'm very well aware of this surgeon's reputation. He has a tendency to curse, yell and throw instruments when things are becoming difficult or not going well. Circulating nurses won't stay in the operating room with him. They will stand outside the OR door until they are needed, for fear of being cursed at, yelled at or hit with a thrown instrument. Residents and students live in fear of being blamed for whatever goes wrong. His reputation had preceded him prior to my arrival and it was quite well known throughout the hospital.

It's 7:30 in the morning and I'm changing into scrubs in the OR locker room when Dr. Williams, the senior ophthalmology resident, enters and starts changing into scrubs. I am already in scrubs, sitting down on the bench with my elbows resting on bent knees with my head in my hands and staring at the floor. Dr. Williams asks, "Are you Ok?" I answer, "It's my first day on general surgery with Dr. Romero." He nods and replies, "Oh, I assume then you must know his reputation?" I nodded yes. He continued to get dressed in scrubs and when completely dressed, he walked over, stopped and stood in front me. I raised my head, leaned back and looked up at him. He asked, "Have you met Dr. Romero?" I shook my head no and said, "I've never met him, I'm supposed to introduce myself this morning as the new student. I'm not even sure that he knows I'm coming." Dr. Williams leans back against one of the lockers and said, "Dr. Romero rotates off of the general surgery teaching service in two weeks and Dr. Anderson rotates on. What would think about working with me for the next two weeks doing admission histories and physicals on my eye surgery patients, along with helping me in the OR which really doesn't amount to doing much other than observing. Then I'll teach you what you need to know about follow up eye care in the hospital. When Dr. Anderson comes on, you can rotate onto the general surgery service, and I'll vouch for you." I couldn't believe my ears and what I had just heard. I said, "You've got a deal!"

After a great two weeks on the eye service, I rotated onto the general surgery teaching service with Dr. Anderson and his surgical resident. I introduced myself to Dr. Anderson, who was a tall physically fit physician in his late fifties with salt and pepper hair who shook my hand and said, "Dr. Williams had some very nice things to say about you. Welcome to our service. You arrived at a perfect time, we were just about to start morning rounds."

The next morning a married couple came in for outpatient surgery. A biopsy of a suspected inguinal lymph node. She was a tall, very pretty, thin female, with blonde hair, blue eyes and an hourglass fiqure. She was wearing a red pill box hat, white blouse, red short open jacket, red skirt and matching red high heel shoes. She was walking beside and holding hands with her husband, a career naval chief petty officer in his dress blue uniform with polished gold colored brass buttons. The pair were a very lovely, majestic looking couple. They had been married for just over nine years with no children. They had been trying with no success but blamed that on him being deployed and gone so often. Her primary care provider had found a lump under her skin just above the right leg abdominal groin crease and wanted it biopsied. It was believed to be an enlarged lymph node and could represent a cancer such as lymphoma. Dr. Anderson explained," We'll give her a mild sedative, then numb up the skin, make a small incision, remove the node and send her home today. It should be very straight forward. We do this on occasion for active-duty families when there is no military base medical facility close."

In the OR Dr. Anderson numbed up the skin, made a small incision, removed the lump and held it in his hand for a few minutes staring at it. He turned to our circulating nurse and said, "I need a specimen container, and I want you to personally take this to the pathologist and tell him I need a stat identification." He stitched the skin closed and we waited. A short time later the circulating nurse returned and whispered something in Dr. Anderson's ear. He then numbed up the skin on the other side just above the left groin crease in a similar place, made a small incision, inserted his index finger into the incision and found a similar lump that he removed. Placed it in a specimen container and told the nurse, "Same stat identification." He told the anesthesiologist to tell the recovery nurse that when the patient was recovered and dressed, we needed to talk to her and her husband in a conference room.

After the skin was closed and dressings were applied, we adjourned to a small conference room. When we walked in behind Dr Anderson, he said, "Close the door." After that we sat down, he slowly said, "Those weren't lymph nodes, they were testicles. This is a case of testicular feminization syndrome. At birth, she would have looked absolutely female and would have been raised as a female. The testicles develop next to the kidneys then migrate down through the abdomen, then through the inguinal canal and into the scrotum before birth. If there is no testosterone then the male genitalia and scrotum do not develop. You get a small, short vagina. No uterus or ovaries but the adrenal glands sitting on top of the kidneys will produce a small amount of estrogen, just enough to cause breast development. How the hell did this get missed until now?" The resident who did the presurgical history said, "Her mother passed away when she was a very young child. Her father was a career military man, and he raised her by himself. They moved from base to base and now she's married to a career military man, and they move from base to base. She said she never gets sick and is on no meds." Dr Anderson asked, " Was there a pelvic exam listed in the information that was sent to us." Resident replied, "No. it looks like she slipped through the cracks. Breaking this to them is going to take some real finesse." I interrupted and said, "I'm sorry to interject this, but I know Navy petty officers and if you tell him he's married to a genetic male, we will destroy their marriage and their last nine years let alone what it will do to her. We took an oath to 'Above all else, do no harm.'" The resident replied, "But not telling them the truth is harmful! They deserve the truth." Dr. Anderson who had been leaning back in his chair with his arms crossed staring down at nothing, looked up and said, "We are going to tell them the truth. When we go in there, I don't want either of you to open your mouth and say a single word. Do you understand?" We both nodded yes.

There was a knock at the door and the circulating nurse entered carrying a lab slip, handed it to Dr. Anderson and she said, "They are ready in the conference room for you." Then she left. Dr Anderson read the slip out loud, "Hypoplastic Glandular Testicular Tissue. So, the testicles never developed, thus no testosterone, no male anatomy and no puberty. Let's go talk to them and remember not a word out of you two." They were in the conference room sitting, leaning towards each other with her right hand being held in between both of his hands with his and her fingers intertwined. They both had a very concerned worried look on their faces. Dr. Anderson smiled and said, "I have good news. We found another lump on the other side, that's why you have two incisions, and both were completely benign. No cancers."

A look of absolute relief appeared on their faces. Her husband softly sighed, "Thank God." Then Dr. Anderson apprehensively said, "I have some not so good news," Then he hesitated for a few moments considering his next words very carefully and said, "We discovered that you have a congenital absence of your uterus. You were born without one, and that explains why you have never had a period. I am also very sorry to tell you this, but without a uterus, it's impossible for you to become pregnant." We saw tears start to well up in her eyes and a single tear ran down her cheek. Her husband kissed the back of her hand and softly said, "It's going to be ok. I love you with all of my heart. We'll be alright." Then Dr. Anderson said, "We'll let your doctor know the results and what we have found. I would also like you to follow up with him in a few days to take the stitches out and see how you are doing." She nodded in agreement. We left the room and closed the door to give them some privacy. Walking down the hall the resident asked, "Do think we did the right thing?" Dr. Anderson replied, "I Hope so. Did you see them? I just couldn't bring myself to destroy that. Was there anything that I said in there that wasn't true?" We both shook our heads no. Then he said, "I'll talk to her doctor to let him know exactly what we did, the things that I said and didn't say, and see if he agrees." The resident asked, "What if someone else finds out and tells them?" Dr. Anderson replied, "That's on that person to decide. I would hope they would use the utmost compassion. I just couldn't do it. They have been happy with each other for at least nine years. If that was your sister and you knew this, would you tell her knowing what it might destroy and what it could do to her emotionally along with what alternative could you offer that would be better?" The resident hesitated for a moment then shook his head no and said, "I think I would take that knowledge to my grave." Dr. Anderson asked, "Then why wouldn't we do the same for her? That person in there was raised female from the day she was born. I couldn't, in good conscience, risk destroying what I saw in that room. I don't know what the future may bring but it's worth taking the chance. Above all else, do no harm should not be just for us but for life in general. I wish them both a happy life. Do you agree?" We both nodded yes. Then he sighed and said, "Well, we still have hospital teaching rounds to make. So, let's go."

I graduated, passed the licensing exam and I got my first job in the small rural community of Lake City Iowa. I thought living close to a lake would be very exciting. We could go fishing, swimming and enjoy the lake. What we found was a small farming community in south western Iowa where there was no lake. I looked everywhere and couldn't find it. I assumed it would be close to the town named Lake City. Had I looked before, I would have seen there was no lake on the map. I asked people where the lake was and the answer was, "What Lake?" There must have been a lake at some time in the past. I did find a small creek running past the town, but I'm guessing "Creek City" didn't sound very enticing.

I had gone to work for the Mcrary-Rost Clinic, covering the clinic, hospital and ER. It was here the skills my father taught me were particularly important and useful. Most important of all, was how to be quiet and listen to what was actually being said without interrupting. People will tell you almost everything you need to know if you just let them. Then ask your questions. It also makes people feel more comfortable when you are genuinely interested in what they are saying, and they are more likely to tell you the more important intimate or embarrassing details of why they were actually here. The first year out of school is a terrifying year because you are doing real medicine on real people by yourself without help. I came to understand that I wasn't taught and didn't learn everything in school. I acquired just enough knowledge to keep my butt out of trouble. The rest I am going to learn on the job. OJT, OMG who would have thought.

On my first day, there was one lesson that they absolutely didn't teach in medical school. There was a very pretty young woman who would dress in the most provocative clothes when she came into the clinic. No one wanted to see her and I soon discovered why. I read in the chart that she had a psychiatric syndrome where she would try to seduce you in the exam room and then scream rape. I was the youngest and newest member of the clinic. The low person on the totem pole. They assigned Her to me. She arrived that day in a short, short black leather skirt. A red blouse that was open down the middle of the front all the way to the top of her skirt and no bra. One of the Docs pulled me aside and said, "Be extremely careful. This is a Honey Trap. It looks sweet but becomes a very sticky situation." That was my first on the job lesson. I begged Kris, my nurse, to go with me into the exam room for my protection. Everyone else stopped, stood and watched with concerned looks on their faces as we entered the exam room door. As if we were walking the last mile on death row. I thought to myself as I entered, "I can always get a job fixing cars." The patient looked at me and she smiled. Then looked at Kris, who walked in behind me, and the smile disappeared. After she left, I thanked Kris for being my bodyguard. Kris said she had two boys and a husband at home so she knows how to handle difficult situations. We later heard that the leather skirt open blouse lady had become a singer that ran away with a country and western band to Nashville. Myself and the whole clinic breathed a collective sigh of relief, but the lessons didn't stop there.

I was a new clinician and practicing in a small town in Iowa. We had our son Robert but our daughter was just a wish and a hope. This was my first real medical job for which I was actually getting paid. On my third day a young couple came in because she was feeling ill for the past several days with nausea, vomiting, light headed and just didn't feel quite right. She thought maybe she had the stomach flu but it seemed to be hanging on. They were a lovely young couple who had been married for just 6 months and you could tell that they were very much in love by the way they looked at each other, the way they held hands and the concern you could see for her in his eyes. He was farming with his elderly dad and would ultimately take over some day. It would be passed down and eventually become his and her farm. In the mean time to help them get on their feet, she was working outside the home. If I remember correctly, she loved her job as the secretary of the elementary school where she thought she had contracted the stomach flu. The two of them were just getting started in life. They had very little and were postponing having children until they were financially more secure. She had gone to the very busy medical residents free clinic an hour away in the city, where she could get a free pap-smear and started on 3 months of free birth control pills. After listening to her history, I did an exam, eyes, ears, mouth, throat, heart, lungs and abdomen but found essentially nothing wrong. I suggested that we get some lab work and a urine specimen for analysis, because a urinary tract or bladder infection is capable of causing this very problem and in newly married couples it is quite common. In fact it's so common, it's called Honeymoon Cystitis and is easily treated with an antibiotic.

After the specimens were all collected, I went into the lab, and a thought crossed my mind. I asked the lab tech to run one additional test. A pregnancy test for completeness sake even though she was on birth control. When the tests were all done, the lab tech looked at me with a strange look on her face and without saying a word, she held up a slip of paper with the word positive printed on it. The pregnancy test was positive. Well this is quite the dilemma. I'm new at this. How do I tell them. It's certainly going to be a surprise. Will they be upset and unhappy when I tell them? Now I'm nervous. I returned to the exam room and asked, "Have you been taking your birth control pills every single day and could you have missed any?" Before she could answer, her husband blurted out, "They were making her sick, so I've been taking them."

It is quite rare that I am speechless, but this was one of those rare occasions. I smiled, nodded my head slightly and sat down trying to think of what to do or say next. I cleared my throat and finally said, " Well, I don't think birth control pills work quite like that and what you have is not the flu. I had the lab run an additional test. A pregnancy test and it's positive. You're going to be a mom and dad." They both had the look of absolute shock on their faces when they turned and looked at each other. That look of absolute surprise turned slowly into smiles, laughter and hugs. To my surprise I even got hugged, which I have decided is one of the nicer perks of this job.

Several months later they became the proud parents of a wonderful baby boy. I learned two lessons that day. One, you can't assume people automatically know everything about what they are taking or even anything about what they are taking. So, we need to explain things better. Two, If a man truly is in love his wife, he will do almost anything for her. Even taking birth control pills that were making her sick. Interestingly enough, he had noticed, that while on the pills, he didn't need to shave near as often. More lessons coming.

I had been working for the clinic and hospital for the past three months when John and Carrie came in. Carrie had been sick for the past week with nausea, vomiting, light headedness and just not feeling quite right. Carrie was 40 and John was 44, they had three girls age 16, 13, and 11. John and Carrie had decided in the past that they were done and didn't want any more children. They had developed a normal family routine that was comfortable. John farmed and Carrie worked at a bank in another small town where she thought she probably picked up the stomach flu. I thought that this was sounding a little familiar and I was starting to have a serious case of de ja vue. So I asked, "Your chart says you're on Ortho birth control pills. Are you still on them?" She answered, "Yes, I never miss taking them. We don't want any more children." John chimed in,"Three girls is enough. The estrogen level in our house is sky high and they all get cranky on the same day."

I was quite relieved to know that he wasn't taking them. I did an exam, eyes, ears, mouth, throat, lungs, heart, abdomen and essentially found nothing wrong. I recommened that we get some blood work and a urine specimen including a pregnancy test. Carrie snorted and said emphatically, "I am not pregnant!" I explained to her that we have to do it for completeness sake as part of the total work up. I was suspecting that this would turn out to be nothing more than some sort of a temporary viral illness. Carrie said looking at her husband, "I had better not be pregnant or you're going to be sleeping in the barn!"

It was a fairly nice spring day and we weren't very busy, so I hung out in the lab while the tests were being run. When done, our lab tech said, "Everything is normal, except one and I ran it twice just to be absolutely certain." She tilted her head and smiled a huge smile then handed me the test slip with the word positive in bold letters printed on it. With slip in hand, I slowly walked over to the closed exam room door and I could hear them talking . "I had better not be pregnant," Carrie mumbled. I opened the door, stepped in and handed Carrie the pregnancy test slip. She looked at the slip then looked up at me and said, " You've got to be kidding!" I said, "No, you're pregnant." She pleaded, "That's not possible. I can't be. I never missed a single pill. I have them right here in my purse." She reached into her purse, pulled out the pills and handed them to me. She said, "If I am, I'm going to sue that company for everything they're worth!" I said, "I am sorry, and you are pregnant but before you do that. We have a pharmacist here today checking our medication cabinet, let me show these to him to see what he thinks." I handed the possibly defective pills to Bill the pharmacist and explained the entire situation. He popped one of the pills out of the pack, rubbed it between his thumb and index finger, then smelled it, and got a very strange look on his face. He said, "Birth control pills, huh. I think, I know what these are but let me get something and I'll be right back." In a few moments Bill walked into the exam room carrying a very large thick book and opened it to a picture. He said, "Your pill has an identification mark on it. The same one as the pill in this picture. Do you see what it says under the picture?" Carrie, seated on a chair, looked at the picture and then looked up at Bill and said, "Aspirin?" Bill said, " If you look at the pack, you can see that it has been tampered with." She quickly turned to her husband and asked, "Have you been taking a lot of aspirin lately?" John answered, "No, I haven't taken any in months, why do ask?" Carrie said, "I thought you had taken them, because a few days ago, I found the aspirin bottle in our medicine cabinet was empty and I was going to get more today while we were in town." Carrie leaned back in her chair and put her left hand over mouth and stared off in to space. John goes, "Oh my God I know that look. She's figured this out." Carrie removed her hand and said, "John, our oldest daughter has a very serious boyfriend. If what I think happened, we are about to have a daughter that is going to be our full time maid, housekeeper, laundress and cook."

She didn't have to explain what she was thinking. We all knew. I interupted and said, "At forty Carrie, you are a high risk patient and we need to get you an appointment with an obstetrician." A little over two weeks later Carrie brought her eldest daughter in for an appointment, an exam and the daughter's own prescription for birth control pills. After the exam I asked the daughter how much hot water she was in. Her answer was, "Not as bad as I deserved. It could have been much worse. I'm actually getting pretty good at house work and cooking with mom." I asked, "How old are you and how serious are you about this young man of your's?" She replied, "I'll be seventeen next week.

He's already seventeen and has a partime job at the hardware store. I love him with all my heart. "I smiled remembering and softly stated, "I started going with my wife when we were sixteen. I do love her so."

A few months later, John and Carrie brought their new baby into their doctor for a well baby check. Curiosity got the better of Kris and I. So, we went down to the pediatric exam room for a visit and to see the new baby. The nurse after weighing the baby, had just laid it down on the exam table and the three sisters now hovering over the baby were all helping to remove it's clothing. When the eldest daughter removed the diaper we had a sudden fountain spraying two feet into the air and John proudly said, "That's my boy." Then sighed and said, "But he's going to be so spoiled and confused with four mothers." Carrie laughed, looked at me, then shrugged her shoulders and said John has never been happier. He has his boy now to help with the farm some day. He's already bought him a toy tractor. She smiled and said, "I guess he was meant to be here. I feel guilty and now that he's here, I can't imagine why I was so upset."

We had a particularly rainy spring that year. It seemed like it rained almost every weekend. Farm fields and parks were constantly wet. Rivers and streams were filled to the brim with water and sometimes they over flowed. With the warm weather and all the moisture, there had developed a heavy over growth of vegetation and weeds. One of which was the dreaded and hated poison ivy. When the oil from this plant's leaves and stems touches your skin, it causes intense itching and inflammation along with a reaction that causes blisters to form in streaks or clusters.

The first patients in the ER that day were a young husband and wife couple in the same exam room. Kris, my nurse said, " They think they have poison ivy." Kris smirked and said, "Wait until you see where." I entered the exam room and said, "Kris says you think you may have poison ivy. May I see it." They removed their clothes that covered the areas involved. She had it diffusely from her lower back extending all the way down the backs of both legs to her ankles. He had it on the front of his legs from his knees on down. I said, " It looks like you're correct. That is poison ivy." She exasperatedly said, " We know and we've tried every cream and ointment we had, showered twice and nothing works. It keeps getting worse. It itches so badly, we can't sleep and I can't sit down." I asked, " What soap did you use?" She answered, "A bar soap that we had." I asked, " What kind of dish soap do you have?" She answered, " Dawn, I think." Her husband sarcastically asked, "What does dish soap have anything to do with this. We just want this to go away." I said, " Until you get the poison ivy plant oils off of your skin, this reaction will not stop and dish soap is one of the best at removing those oils. So, I want both of you to go home and shower with the Dawn dish soap. You may have to do it 2 days in a row. Once the oils are gone it will stop this ongoing reaction and it will start getting better. I'm also going to start you on some oral antihistamines and oral steroids to decrease the itching and calm down the inflammation. You should be able to get some sleep but it won't start getting better until you get the oils off of your skin." He answered with a sigh, "OK, we can do that."

A few days later a male science teacher and coach walked in very awkwardly with his legs spread apart moving very slowly. Kris said, "He wouldn't sit down to let me take his vital signs and when I asked what he was here about, He said he would like to explain it to just you. His wife came along because she had to do the driving and is in there with him looking quite concerned. I don't think they have started summer sports at school yet, so that rules out a few possibilities. If it's alright with you, I don't think I am going to go in there with you on this one. You can always yell for help if you need me."

I entered the exam room and without saying a word he unzipped and lowered his trousers. I know we are trained to be stoic but my eyes got large and I said, "Oh my lord. This is definitely going to require some explaining." He explained that they live on 5 acres out in the country. There is a grove of trees on the edge of their property that works as a partial wind break. He had gone out after breakfast to clear weeds and brush out of the grove. To protect his hands from being cut or scraped, he wore a pair of thick cotton gloves. He admitted that he had unfortunately drank several cups of coffee that morning and suddenly had to go very urgently. So, being all alone, he removed his gloves and quickly relieved himself behind a tree. Put the gloves back on and he finished weeding the grove. After he was done, he went into the house and washed the sap off of his hands at the kitchen sink that had penetrated through the cotton gloves. Last night after supper, he started to itch down there and early this morning when the intense itching woke him up, he noticed it was very swollen and getting larger. He said, "This morning , because of what I suspected, I went out to the brush pile to be burned and I could see a few poison ivy leaves in there. So, I'm assuming this is from poison ivy but why is it not on my hands?" I asked, " What was the soap you washed your hands with?" His wife said, "It's Joy dish soap in a squeeze bottle that I keep on the back of the sink because he frequently has grease on his hands from working on his old tractor." I asked, "Can you still pee and if you can, does it hurt? He answered, "Yes I can and no it doesn't." I said, "Then I agree that it's most likely to be swollen from a reaction to the poison ivy. I need you to go home and shower with the Joy dish soap and concentrate on getting the oils off of the swollen area. I also am going to start you on some oral antihistamines and oral steroids to reduce itching and inflammation. I want to see you tomorrow for a recheck. He had this pleading look on his face and asked, "It's not going to be permanently damaged is it?" I answered, "No, I really don't think so. See you tomorrow." The next day it was slightly smaller and he was feeling a little better. So, we released him to follow up with his primary care provider.

It's late summer and a very lovely warm sunny morning. I thought to myself, "It's such a nice day. What could possibly go wrong on a nice day like this." An elderly gentleman walked in wearing shorts, a short sleeve shirt and a wide brimmed straw hat with a shark emblem on the hat band. He complained of an itchy rash on his arms and legs. He told Kris, "My wife made me come in. She thinks I have fleas. I don't have fleas." His very weathered sun tanned skin had a rash from his knees down to the top of his socks and stopped there abruptly. It was also from his elbows down to and stopped at his wrists. His hands had tan lines consistent with perforated leather baseball or golf gloves. At his age, I doubted baseball. I said, "I'm guessing you're a golfer?" He replied, "Yes I am. I'm not that good but I really enjoy the game. I lose a few balls in the weeds now and then but not too bad."

Looking at the rash I asked, "Did you play golf yesterday? He nodded yes. And the rash started last night? Again he nodded yes. Does your wife have a rash? He shook his head no. Then what you have is not fleas. It's poison ivy from rummaging around in the weeds at the golf course." He said, "Well that makes more sense than fleas, we don't have any animals." I said, "I can't put you on any antihistamines for the itching because at your age it could shut off your urine and you wouldn't be able to pee. He replied, "My urologist told me the same thing and that I shouldn't take those." I reassured him, "We can help get rid of this by starting you on a low dose steroid cream to apply daily to the rash but most importantly, I need you to go home today and shower with Dawn or Joy." He hesitated for a moment then got a strange look on his face and sheepishly said, "I don't think my wife will approve." I replied, "What, you don't think she will approve of you taking a shower with Dawn or Joy?" Kris, who was leaning against the wall behind me listening, interrupted and said, "Les, repeat what you just said a minute ago." I answered, "You mean about the part that his wife won't approve of him taking a shower with dish soap?" Kris replied, "No, the part where you said, I need you to go home today and shower with Dawn or Joy!"

As what she had just said sunk in, I had an epiphany at that very instant. It sounded so incredibly different when someone else said it, but I knew what it meant to me when I said it. It's possible that we may not all be on the same wave length. I gasped, "Oh my God Kris, do you know how many people I've said that to this summer." I turned back to our elderly gentleman, reassured him that the cream and showering with dish soap will help and that I certainly didn't intend to convey in any way shape or form that he should shower with someone named Dawn or Joy. He smiled. I was quite embarrassed. He left smiling and we could hear him chuckling to himself as he walked out the door.

A few days later, Kris and I were sitting at the nurses station when the phone rang. Kris picked it up and listened intently. After listening for a short while, she said, "Let me have you speak to him." She put her hand over the receiver, looked at me, tilted her head, smiled then sarcastically said, "This call is for you. Definitely for you." I cringed when I took the receiver and said, "Hello?" On the other end was a female voice that angrily said, "Did you tell my husband that he had to shower with somebody named Dawn or Joy!" I fudgingly and timidly explained, "No, I told him to shower with Dawn or Joy dish soap to help get rid of his rash." I heard her turn away and yell at her poor husband, "Martin, you moron, he meant dish soap!" She turned back to the phone and said, "Thank you, just checking have a wonderful day." and hung up. I turned to Kris and embarrassedly said, "This is going to get all around town isn't it." Kris leaned back in her chair and smiled. Just nodded and smiled.

It was a beautiful summer day, partly cloudy with the warm sun peaking through the clouds just enough to feel the warmth on my face. I was sitting on the cool cement steps outside of the clinic entrance drinking a cup of coffee. I was just enjoying the morning, watching and waving at people as they go by on their way to work plus children riding their bikes, laughing and playing in the small park on the town square. It's amazing how this kind of weather on a beautiful summer morning causes the clinic and ER to have a very rare slow day. I was sitting there thinking about how nice it will be to actually have time for lunch at the restaurant on the other side of the square with my wife Donette. Having lunch with her is one of my most favorite things to do but it happens so rarely. I do love her so.

Kris, my nurse stepped outside, touched my shoulder with her hand and said, "You have a phone call on line one." I looked up at her and said, "Do you know who it is?" Kris replied, "It's Mrs. Williams and she's hotter than a pistol." I sighed and said, "Great. I suspected this might happen."

Back in my office, I took a deep breath and pushed the lighted button for line one on the phone. I picked up the receiver and said, "This is Les Newhouse, good morning Mrs. Williams, how can I help you?" Mrs. Williams screamed into her phone, "HOW DARE YOU. HOW DARE YOU PRESCRIBE BIRTH CONTROL PILLS TO MY DAUGHTER WITHOUT MY PERMISSION. I SAW HER OPEN PURSE THIS MORNING ON THE KITCHEN COUNTER AND THERE WERE BIRTH CONTROL PILLS LAYING INSIDE IT. I PICKED THEM UP AND YOUR NAME WAS ON THEM AS THE PRESCRIBER. HOW DARE YOU GIVE THEM TO HER. THAT SAYS TO EVERYONE THAT YOU THINK IT'S ALRIGHT FOR HER TO HAVE SEX AS A CHILD."

She was yelling so loud, that I had to move the receiver away from my ear and I could still hear her quite plainly. After a 5 minute rant, there at last finally appeared a quiet moment when she ran out of things to yell. I moved the phone back up to my ear and asked, "Are you finished so we can calmly discuss this?" There was just quiet on the other end of the phone, except I could still hear her deep breathing. I said, "I'm going to assume that since you're being quiet that your answer is yes. Have you by any chance discussed this with your daughter?" She answered, "No, we've grounded her to her room." I replied, "Yeah, that's really going to work. I had a long discussion with your daughter at her appointment, so I know she is a straight A student, has a part time job at the restaurant on the square as a waitress and volunteers as a Candy Striper in the obstetrics department at the hospital. She is a very remarkable young woman and that is the right terminology. She just turned 17 and is a young woman. She told me that she had fallen very much in love with a wonderful young man that is in high school with her and that he is deeply in love with her also. I just happen to know him quite well and he is a fine young man who is also an A student and works very hard on his parent's farm with his dad. Both he and your daughter have aspirations of going to college and a child would be a big problem right now. Your daughter has made plans for her future and wants to become a nurse. I happen to know that she saved her waitress money, made the appointment on her own, paid for the appointment with her own money and endured a very embarrassing first time examination. Girls who don't need birth control pills wouldn't do that. She told me that she knows that teenage romances sometimes don't always work out and she doesn't want to end up being a single mother struggling on welfare or having to ask for an abortion which would mean that your first grandchild would cease to exist." Mrs Williams asks, "Couldn't you have talked her out of it?" I replied, "Could anyone have talked you out of it? She knows that you were pregnant with her on the day that you and her father were married." Mrs Williams asks, "How did she find out?" I answered, "She is a very smart young lady, she saw her birth certificate with her weight of 8 pounds and 6 ounces. She counted just under 7 months from your wedding day to her birthday. By volunteering and helping the nurses in the hospital obstetrics unit, she knows that a 2 month premature baby doesn't weigh 8 pounds and 6 ounces. She said she loves you very much as her mother but does not want this to happen to her. She knows how much you gave up and sacrificed for her and she loves you for it. So, grounding her to her room at her age may not have been the wisest choice. She could easily become frustrated and angry with you for treating her like a child, because she doesn't see herself as a child. She said that you still think of her as a child but when she looks at herself in the mirror, she doesn't see a child, she sees a grown woman with feelings of a grown woman. I also happen to know that her young man has a very nice car and they could very easily run away together. It's possible that you could lose her, because being in love is very emotional, not logical and I have seen people do some very strange things for love.

You have some very tough choices to make. If I may ask, do you know what you're going to do?" I could hear her sniffling when she answered, " Right now, I need a tissue to go blow my nose." When she returned she said, "I'm not sure. I didn't think it would be this hard. I was just very angry at you." I calmly added, "May I make a suggestion, if it was me and my daughter, I would go in, sit down with her, put my arms around her and the first words out of my mouth would be, I Love You So Very Much and I'm Sorry, then ask her to invite her young man over for supper some evening so you can meet and get to know him. I think you will be amazed at the response you'll get from your daughter. She is a most remarkable young woman and you did a great job with her. You're a great mom. After that I'm sure you can figure out what to say next. My suggestion would be, I Love You, as much as possible. We don't say that nearly often enough. Children who hear I Love You frequently from their parents have a tendency to actually listen to their parents even if they don't show it at the time. Your daughter is going to have important grown up questions that she will need answers to from someone she trusts who loves her. There is no one more important in a daughter's life, than her mom. If it doesn't work out, and they decide to go their separate ways, you'll be there to support her. That's what moms do."

She was very quiet on the other end of the phone for a few moments and then quietly said, "Thank you. I will have to explain this to my husband, he's a very black or white right or wrong kind of guy. No in-between, but I'm sure he will understand. I will give the pills back to her. I'm sorry that I yelled at you." I replied, "It's OK. If I can't defend what I'm doing then I shouldn't be doing it." Then she said, "Would you like to help us with our 13 year old son? He's driving my poor husband crazy." I said, "I'm sure you will do just fine. You're a great mom." She hung up her phone and the conversation ended. When Kris heard me hang up, she poked her head into the room and said, Our first patient is ready. Wait until you see this one. It's a little kid who stuffed a foam Nerf ball up his nose and mom can't get it out."

It was Friday night and my night to cover the ER. Friday nights are historically the night of injuries, the unusual and the strange. It's football games, basketball, Proms, people having one or more cold ones for the end of the work week and fights. Then there was the full moon this night. It seems to bring out all the strangeness in people.

The first patient of the night arrived complaining of abdominal pain. She was a large young woman, 5 feet 11 inches tall and approximately 210 to 220 pounds with light brown hair and a very pale complexion befitting someone who is in pain. I overheard her tell the receptionist that she had a history of kidney stones and this feels very similar. After getting registered, she asked the receptionist, "I need to use the restroom in a hurry, is there one close?" The receptionist pointed to the one just inside the ER door only a few feet away, then said, "If the door is closed be sure to knock. There is no lock on that door."

My nurse Connie and I were sitting at the nurses station waiting for her to come out when we heard the most ear splitting, horror sounding, blood curdling scream coming from inside that restroom. The nurse bolted for the restroom door and opened it. She found our patient standing, and straddling the toilet beneath her with an umbilical cord protruding from between her legs attached to a baby that was head down in the toilet. The nurse screamed, grabbed the baby out of the toilet, we clamped and cut the cord then raced to the closest exam room. The baby was blue and not breathing. We started CPR and the nurse grabbed a neonatal ambu bag and started forcing breaths into the baby's lungs while I did compressions on the chest. Within a few moments the baby coughed started breathing and crying. That sound was absolute music to our ears. The baby's hands and feet were extremely blue and were the last to finally pink up. I examined the baby from head to toe. Eyes bright, good cry, lungs clear, good heart beat and actively moving both arms and legs. Now, I could breath normally. I stayed with the baby while Connie ordered a baby warmer on wheels and help from obstetrics.

When Connie returned, I glanced around the ER and noticed that we were the only ones there, then said, "Connie, where's mom?" Connie glanced around the ER, then her eyes became large and without saying a word she ran to the restroom. She stuck her head out of the restroom door and yelled, "She's sitting on the toilet, leaning against the wall and unconscious. She has a good pulse and is breathing. Looks like she fainted and I can't move her." I yelled back, "Page over head for 4 big strong men stat to the ER restroom." Almost instantly 2 maintenance men who were fixing a plumbing leak, an orderly off of the main hospital floor and Peter, a family practice doc still wearing his bicycle helmet, appeared at the restroom. Peter popped his head out of the door and yelled, "She has a good pulse, blood pressure and breathing are fine. It appears she fainted." Each one of them grabbed an arm or a leg while Connie supported her head as they carried her out through the restroom door to an awaiting gurney then quickly into an exam room. Peter said, "I'll take care of her if you like." I said, " Be my guest and thank you for coming." The obstetric nurse had arrived and started an IV in mom. Suddenly we heard another blood curdling scream. I asked, "Is everything ok?" Peter replied, "Yes, she just woke up."Peter delivered the placenta and proceeded to get everything stabilized.

I finally had some time to look at her chart and found out that her name was Angela. I said to Peter, "Let me know when it's OK to bring the warmer over." Peter replied, "We're doing fine. I think it's OK now. Connie and I wheeled the warmer around the corner and into Angela's room. I said, "Angela, let me introduce you to your brand new daughter." We could see tears start to well up in her eyes, a smile appear on her face and Angela started to cry. She stretched out her arm and touched the baby's soft hand that automatically wrapped her tiny fingers around mom's index finger and held on. After a few moments I asked Angela, "Did someone bring you here?" She answered, "Yes, my husband. I'm sure he is in the waiting room or outside." With a concerned look on her face she said, "He has a phobia about hospitals. He passes out at the sight of blood and if someone is throwing up, he's right there throwing up with them." "So you're saying that I should bring him back in a wheelchair," I replied. I walked out to the waiting room and there was no one there. I asked the receptionist and she pointed to the hospital entrance. Through the glass double doors, I could see him nervously pacing back and forth outside. When he saw me, he quickly came back in and said, "How's my wife, is she alright?" I said , "She's fine. In fact the problem has been completely resolved and she wants to see you." He asked, "What was wrong. Was it a kidney stone?" I replied, "I think it's best that your wife explains this."

I wheeled him back to see her in a wheelchair which was much to his chagrin and complaining about being required to be in the chair. Everyone had left the room and pulled the curtain closed to give them some privacy. Mom was now holding her new daughter. I wheeled him in, then immediately left and stood just outside the curtain just in case. I heard through the curtain a soft, "Oh my God." Then a few moments later, "She's beautiful." That's when I knew we were OK.

Peter agreed to take care of them in the hospital and be their doctor. We found out later that she had irregular periods throughout her teenage years and adult life, and would sometimes miss periods for a few months. With the new jobs, the move here and eating out a great deal, she thought that was the cause of her weight gain. So, she didn't think this was anything unusual until the pain started. She had been told by her previous doctor, that because of the irregular periods, the random chance of her having children was highly unlikely. So, that thought never crossed her mind. They were both teachers and had taken new jobs for this upcoming fall. He taught History and she taught English. What we feared may happen, didn't happen. He didn't pass out when he saw his new daughter or throw up. He became a dad and whether you want to believe it or not, love does strange things that changes you inside.

I found this to be an extremely rare occasion in the ER, where chaos and terror can remarkably change into joy and happiness right before your very eyes. Although, we would still like to know how he handles it when his daughter has that first major blowout diaper. I'm guessing, that this dad will do just fine. I wonder if they will ever tell her, that she was born in a toilet. Probably not.

Late one afternoon, one of the local business owners came into the clinic. She owned a fashionable nice little dress shop that was doing very well. The high heel on her shoe caught in a sidewalk grate while walking to work and had broken the day before. She had fallen and twisted her ankle. Her right ankle was quite swollen, black and blue from bruising along with being painful when she walked. She was sitting on the end of the exam table with her legs hanging down. I was on the short stool below holding her foot and ankle in my hands to examine it. My brain and mouth are sometimes not in sync. I think much faster than I can speak and things come out sometimes not as I had planned. What I meant to say was, we need to get an x-ray and if it's not broken, I will wrap your ankle or tape your ankle which ever works the best. What actually came out of my mouth was, "We need to get an x-ray and if it is not broken I will "wrape" your ankle."

I was shocked, stunned and speechless at what I had just heard myself say. I could not believe what had just happened. I could feel my face getting hot as it turned bright red from embarrassment. I looked up at her. Her eyes were wide open with a shocked look on her face. I hastily tried to explain what had just happened and that I had intended to either wrap or tape the ankle and I put those two words together that came out sounding like something totally unintended. She started to laugh and said, "You should see how red your face is." She laughed so hard she fell backwards on the exam table. When she sat up, she had tears streaming down her face from laughing so hard. I handed her a tissue and as she wiped her face then threw the tissue into the garbage, I could see my career being thrown in there also. I didn't get an x-ray. I taped up the ankle and it worked fine. She walked out of the clinic door still laughing as she left. Kris asked, What's so funny?" I told her the story hoping for some understanding. She laughed so hard she had to sit down. I said, "It's not funny! I'm in trouble!" Kris regained her composure and stopped laughing. Then she looked at me and said, "Yes, it is!" and started laughing again.

That night at supper I thought I had better explain to Donette what had happened at the clinic in case people started staring at her and talking. I told her the whole story from the very beginning while we were eating. She decided to take a drink of milk at the exact moment in the story where I said "Wrape your ankle." She choked, gagged, coughed and had milk bubbling and streaming out of her nose. Robert sat there looking at his mother and smiling because for once it wasn't him with milk coming out of his nose. Donette got up and went into the kitchen for a towel. I could hear laughing coming from out there. I shouted, "Why does everyone think this is so funny? I'm watching my career go down the drain and it's only just gotten started. People will point and say, there goes the guy that wrapes ankles. I could lose my job, and we'll have to move." Then I said, "I know what I'll do. I'll dye my hair, grow a mustache and a beard. Maybe no one will notice me." Donette came out of the kitchen and said, "I don't think it's going to be that bad. It is a bit embarrassing though, but I think we can weather it. If we have to move, we'll move. It's not a big deal." I felt a little better, but I still decided to grow the mustache and beard.

Things at work were not normal for about a week until everyone had used up all the jokes they could think of at my expense and there were quite a few. Over the next few weeks, I noticed that I was seeing more and more injuries, sprained ankles, sprained wrists, wrenched knees, injured shoulders and sports injuries. In light of what had happened, I thought this was very strange. One day I was examining a 17-year-old with a sprained ankle from football, and I told him I was going to tape up his ankle. He said, "Aren't you going to say something funny?" I replied, "I don't think so. Why?" He said, "The lady over at the dress shop tells everyone her story about you and they all think it's really funny. Almost as funny as Mrs. Olsen chasing her naked husband out of the house into the barn with a hot curling iron." I replied, "I didn't hear about this. Which Olsen family? He said, "The one that comes here with the 13 kids. I overheard mom tell dad it was to convince him to get something done." Wanting to change the subject, I said, "Let's get you taped up and no gym or sports until I see you in a week." He said, "OK."

Life is definitely strange. This isn't what I had expected at all. Injuries and sports medicine became a major part of my practice. No one pointed at me and we didn't have to move. I kept the beard and mustache because Donette thought it made me look distinguished. She was my conscience and my stability. I loved her with all my heart.

Donette had applied and became the Special Ed school bus driver. She loves the job and the kids love her. She gets hugs every day when the kids leave the tiny yellow school bus. She looks forward to being with them every morning. Some of the kids have quite serious conditions and need her help getting on and off the bus. Some days they need someone with a warm heart, a compassionate ear to listen and give them a hug when the day doesn't go well. She had become quite attached to them. It was a perfect job for Donette. She loved all children no matter what.

We hadn't lived there very long when Donette developed health problems requiring abdominal surgery. They removed an ovary and its fallopian tube. The tube that takes the egg from the ovary to meet a sperm to begin a new life. It had to be removed because of a benign mass the size of a tennis ball that had developed on one of the ovaries and attached itself to the tube. She recovered quickly but seven days after surgery, the day she was to come home, Donette developed a twisted bowel. An obstruction that doubled her up and she screamed in severe pain. This required urgent surgery which was followed by a pulmonary embolus, a blood clot to her lung, that kept her 9 days in the intensive care unit on blood thinners and oxygen followed by another week of recovery in the hospital. I had almost lost her. After all of this, as if all of what she had just gone through wasn't enough, we were told by two different doctors that we would never have any more children. The process that caused the mass would prevent it. Life does not care what your hopes and dreams are. It can sometimes be cruel and Donette was devastated. We had planned on having four children. She thought that would be the perfect number. That was not to be, and she was very thankful that we had our son. We were reconciled to the fact that it was going to be just the three of us.

This is when the hugging began. Donette's family were huggers, my family was not. There was no show of affection in my childhood family. I don't remember my parents ever hugging us or each other. Maybe I just wasn't paying attention, it wasn't that important to me at the time. I'm sure my parents must have hugged at some time in their life. My grandmother was a hugger. She would wrap her arms around me and squeeze. As a child, I would stand stiff, close my eyes and grimace with my arms and hands plastered to my sides. I didn't know what to do with my arms and hands. I had no experience to know where to put them. I didn't want to put them where they weren't supposed to be. It was awkward and how do you ask someone where your hands should be. As an adult, our three-person family hugs did what hugs are supposed to do. Rob would see his mother sad, then motion to both of us to pick him up. They made Donette feel better when she was sad and I didn't have to worry about where to put my arms and hands, they fit perfectly around Donette and Robert. The family hugs were very comforting and I would grow to miss them.

A little over a year later, in mid-September, on a routine warm sunny Saturday morning I was getting ready at home to go make rounds at the hospital. I was bent down on one knee tying my shoes when Donette came to me and said, "I'm pregnant." I looked up and said, "No you're not." The conversation goes. "Yes, I am." "No, you're not." "Yes, I am!" I stood up and said, "No, you're not. I know how badly you want to have more children and I'm sorry, but we were told by two different doctors we would never have any more children." Donette said, "I don't care what they said. I'm pregnant!" I said, "Ok fine, let's stop at the clinic and we'll do a pregnancy test." There was no one there at that time in the morning so I could do it quietly myself so as not to embarrass her.

Pregnancy tests in those days required mixing reagents together on a large glass slide. I mixed the reagents together with Donette's sample. It was positive. I must have done something wrong. I was sure I had to have done something wrong. I read the directions. Checked the expiration dates of the reagents. I repeated it twice. It was still positive! Donette grinned at me with the look that said, "I told you so." I was still absolutely sure I must have done something wrong. There had to be something else that I had missed. I left everything on the lab counter for Sherry, our lab tech, with a note that said, "Please run this and call me at the hospital with the results." Sherry called me and said "congratulations." Donette and I were ecstatic and I was afraid at the same time. Sometimes knowledge can be terrifying. I knew what Donette had gone through and I knew what could go wrong. I dare not mention any of this to her. I would keep it totally to myself. I was also quite embarrassed that I had doubted her and it would not happen again.

When our son was born there were no classes we had to attend. Now there were birthing classes, tours of the hospital obstetrics wing, breast-feeding instruction classes and fathers were required to attend. So, I reluctantly went. The first birthing class we attended, I obviously made the nurse teaching the class uncomfortable. After seeing me, she hesitantly stuttered and stammered as if she didn't quite know what to say. We worked together at the hospital and she didn't know I was coming. She assumed that I knew all of this and may know it better than she did. Which I didn't. In fact, it was an area that was not really taught in school and what little was taught, I had actually avoided it. After explaining this to her and that I would be just a normal father, she was more at ease and comfortable. I was told that I was going to be Donette's "birthing coach." We learned how to breath when she had a contraction and I was to coach her through it. I learned how to do back massage to relieve her pain along with how to help her concentrate and help her to relax. We became very good at it. We practiced at home. I WAS PARTICIPATING! Donette said I didn't have to attend the breast feeding classes because I was only partially participating.

Several months later, one spring afternoon in 1978, Donette called me at the clinic and said it's time. We had two previous false starts so I finished my charts and calmly drove home. We lived 6 miles out in the country on 5 acres surrounded by newly planted corn and soybean fields. When I arrived home, I was met at the door by a frantic lady with a small suitcase in her hand, shouting, "Where have you been?" It immediately dawned on me that this was the real thing. She hadn't looked this anxious in either of the two previous episodes. I had managed to avoid doing deliveries in my training because I really didn't care for doing obstetrics. I had seen many deliveries and I much preferred resuscitating the infant after someone else delivered it. I just wasn't interested in doing them. Worried now that I may have to do a delivery and at home terrified me. With fear in my voice, I asked how far apart were the contractions? Five minutes was the answer. I quickly put Donette and Robert in the car and we nervously raced off towards the hospital. Donette had just finished a contraction when we left home. I had five minutes to get her to the hospital and we both sincerely hoped I could do it. On the way Donette said, "We haven't picked out a name yet." I said, "We need a name for the birth certificate." We started throwing around a dozen or more girls names, because somehow Donette knew we were having a daughter. I had learned from past experience not to doubt her. None of the names seemed to fit. Robert, now 8 years old, sitting quietly in the back seat said, "How about Bethany?" Donette and I became quiet. She thought about it for a moment and said, "We could call her Bethany Jo. That fits." The name Jo is Gaelic for sweetheart.

We arrived at the hospital where Donette's water immediately broke. A frantic twenty minutes later without prep her doctor, who lived on a farm, rushed in and caught our daughter with his bare hands. There was no prep, no anesthetic, no numbing or pain medication given. After months of both of us worrying about the pregnancy and what Donette had been through. We now had our miracle baby girl named Bethany Jo for sweetheart. No coaching, no breathing and no participating again but at least I was in the delivery room this time. Donette reached up, pulled my face to Her's and gave me a kiss. This was much better than one of the deliveries I had observed as a student. Where the wife reached up, put her hands around her husband's neck and started to strangle him. She pulled his face down in front of her face and screamed, "You did this to me you ###!" I loved my family with all my heart. My delivery record remained intact, zero.

In later years my parents got divorced. As some people do, they evolved in different directions. I was grown up and married at that time but it still affected me. They were my family and now it was broken. I felt a sense of loss. Like a ladder had been kicked out from beneath me. I was slightly angry at them for not trying to work things out. They had been married for 27 years. Had five children. They must have loved each other at one time. My father went to work for the post office. My mother went to the bank, took out a loan, bought a semi-truck and became an independent long-haul trucker. I'm not sure if women go through a mid-life crisis but I think this would qualify. There were extremely few women truckers in those days. She was known throughout the Midwest by the other independent truckers, who would humorously refer to her over the CB radio, as the "Mother Trucker." It was a play on words but meant as a funny compliment. They knew if they needed a helping hand she was always there. They also knew she wouldn't hesitate to scold them, like a mother would, if they did something not very bright. When the recession hit and many truckers went broke, she went back to driving school bus. There were five of us brothers and sisters, three boys and two girls. We all have stories of our mother that would bring a smile to our faces or have us shaking our heads. At 89 she was still a unique individual, speaking her mind and driving us crazy. She lived life on her terms and just as quickly passed away on her terms. Heaven is in for some very real excitement.

In 1979 we had a chance to move to the Black Hills of South Dakota. A significant change from the farmland plains of south western Iowa. I went to work for the Homestake Gold Mine, in Lead South Dakota, in their very busy Emergency Department. The town name is pronounced leed but spelled like lead. The lead load is the first load of ore out of the mine that has the mineral you're looking for, in this case gold. It was a wild west mining town in those days. People getting drunk, having fights, shooting and stabbing each other. Blowing themselves up in the mine, falling off of mountains, and being attacked by wild animals. Real cowboys that were tending large herds of cattle. For a person like me whose childhood heroes were movie cowboys like the Lone Ranger, Hop a Long Cassidy, Roy Rogers and Dale Evans.

The Black Hills was great place to live. It was steeped in wild west history. The question became, "Is it a good place to raise a family?"

When we first moved to the Black Hills of South Dakota, I moved into a temporary apartment and Donette, Robert and Bethany came later. The apartment was owned by the Homestake clinic, it was right on main street in the town of Lead. It was just one block up the street from the clinic, and up is the correct term because no matter where you went in Lead, it was either uphill or down. The apartment building was made of wood construction built in the early 1900s and in the back was a small parking area where one of the black hills sloped away from and towered above the apartment building. The apartments were all on the second floor with tourist and clothing businesses down below on the ground floor with front doors that opened out on to the main street. To enter the apartment building, there was a single ugly wooden door painted white with a black door knob right on main street between two stores. It opened to very steep poorly lighted unpainted wooden steps inside the building that led you up to a narrow dimly lit common hallway and the apartment doors. The apartments had been renovated in the mid to late 1950s with what was then modern bathrooms and kitchens with fixtures that were reminiscent of when I was a child. Avocado green bathtub and sink with matching refrigerator and stove. It was a clean comfortable two-bedroom apartment that came completely furnished even down to towels, dishes and silverware.

The next day was my first day of actual work. I left the apartment for the short walk down main street to the clinic. Half way down the main street sidewalk there was a pair of what I thought were rather large lady's silky white underwear lying on the sidewalk that I had to step over. Several possibilities flashed through my mind for why such a thing would be lying there. None of them I would consider a reasonable logical thought. What kind of town is this? What have we moved into? I entered into the clinic through the emergency room door to find all of the nurses standing in a group surrounding nurse Susan like a herd of wild animals guarding their young. The clinic nurses were very old school and wore nurses' caps, dresses, anklet socks and white shoes. I wondered why they were in a group around Susan. I asked, "What's going on?" One of the nurses replied, "We are waiting for Susan's husband." I inquired, "You're guarding Susan? Is there something I should be worried about?" The answer was, "No he's bringing her a package." I said, "Then why does she need to be guarded if he's only bringing her a package?" I leaned my head over to one side to look at Susan through the wall of nurses. Her face was bright red and she wouldn't make eye contact which was a clue to this mystery. I asked, "Does this have anything to do with what I saw outside on the sidewalk?" Susan looked at me and said, "Oh my God, you saw that!" I unconsciously pointed at the emergency room door and sheepishly replied, "I couldn't miss it. I had to step over it."

Susan then explained that this was her first day back from maternity leave, and that she had tried to not buy expensive maternity clothes. This morning all she had was her stretched out skivves to put on and hoped they would work. While walking quickly down main street to work, they suddenly dropped down around her ankles in front of everyone else on their way to work. She hurriedly, without missing step, stepped out of them leaving the offending garment behind on the sidewalk and briskly entered the clinic. Susan, looking at me with pleading eyes said, "I am so embarrassed! Would you please go out and remove them?" I said, "Why me? Couldn't your husband do that when he gets here?" If glaring was an Olympic event, the team that stood before me would win a gold medal. I reluctantly said, "OK. Fine." I poked my head out of the emergency room door and looked up the sidewalk for the offending garment. It was gone. I was relieved, smiled, pulled my head back in and said, "Good news! It's gone. I'm sure someone picked it up, a dog ran off with it or something." Susan sighed and slowly shook her head back and forth. Someone yelled at me, "You're not helping!" At that moment, thank goodness, her husband arrived with the package and they adjourned to the restroom. I asked if there were any patients that needed to be seen, the answer from the head nurse was, "No, thank goodness."

First day on any job, is never what you expect it to be. I needed coffee. I asked the head nurse where I could get a cup. She said, "The coffee pot and cups are over there," pointing to a small alcove with a sink designed for just such items. I looked at the pot sitting on the cabinet beside the sink and it was filthy. It was a tall stainless steel pot with a spigot at the bottom. It looked like it had not been cleaned in weeks or maybe months. There were brushes hanging on pegs over the sink so I grabbed one and began scrubbing the pot inside and out with soap and hot water. After cleaning, I made a pot of coffee and began slowly sipping the fresh cup of hot coffee. The head nurse walked over, picked up a cup to pour herself some coffee and said, " The pot looks nice and clean." I said, "Yes, I scrubbed it out with that brush," pointing to the brush that I had just used hanging on its peg still dripping water. She put her coffee cup back down, looked at the brush, then at me and asked pointing timidly with her index finger, "That brush?" Being rather proud of myself at how clean the pot looked I said, "Yes." She closed her eyes and then quietly said, "That's the vaginal speculum cleaning brush." I promptly dumped my coffee in the sink. I excused myself, exited through the emergency room door, walked up the street to Pamida, bought bottle of Listerine and a new coffee pot. I sincerely hoped tomorrow would be a better day.

One Saturday morning when I was taking the trash out of the apartment through the narrow common hallway and down the back staircase to the trash bin in the parking area. I bumped into our next-door neighbor taking her trash to the bin. She was a small thin elderly woman in blue jeans wearing a man's western shirt, with mother of pearl snaps instead of buttons, and her pure white hair pulled back into a pony tail. She frankly said, "Hello neighbor, my name is Dolly Perkins, so who are you and what do you do?" I explained who I was and that I was in the Homestake Clinic emergency room. She said, "I just put a pot of coffee on the stove and baked some biscuits if you want a cup and you can tell me all about it." I replied, "I could use a cup of coffee." I followed her upstairs, sat down at her kitchen table and watched as she poured me a cup of coffee and placed some baking powder biscuits with white powdered sugar frosting on the table. In my mind's eye, I could picture her with a colt peacemaker holstered on her hip, cowboy hat and driving a buckboard with team of horses Calamity Jane style. She poured herself a cup and sat down at the kitchen table across from me. It's either what I do for a living or I have a kind face that makes people want to tell me their life story. It turns out my Calamity Jane impression was all wrong. She was originally from northern California and wine country. I asked, "how did you end up in Lead South Dakota?" She wrapped both hands around her warm coffee cup, took a sip and replied, "It's a long story. Your wife is going to think I mugged you at the trash bin." I said, "No, she, our son and daughter went to the grocery store, so I have a little time before they arrive home and you have the coffee and biscuits. It's hard to turn those down"

I learned that Dolly's sister, who was married and lived in Lead with her husband, had developed cancer. Dolly had come all the way from California by train to Denver where her brother-in-law picked her up. She came to spend time with and help care for her sister. After the sister passed away, she helped her brother-in-law with funeral arrangements and all of the legal paperwork afterwards. She was there for a total of several weeks. Just how many, she didn't remember exactly but it was quite a few. The night before she was to catch the train for California, she made herself and her brother-in-law supper. Sitting at the kitchen table he said, "I can't thank you enough for being here and helping. You were truly a God send. You know, you and your sister are so very much alike. I loved your sister very much. I really don't want you to leave. I think you and I would get along famously if you're a mind too." Dolly got very upset with him as her sister had just passed away and she let him know it. How dare he ask such a thing. He took her to the Denver train station the next day and not a word was spoken on the trip. A few days after she arrived home in California, she received a letter from her brother-in-law. He apologised in the letter. The next day another letter came. The day after that another and then another. He wrote her a letter every day for a year. On letter 365 she wrote him a letter with just one word, "YES." Dolly took a sip of her coffee and then a very comforting smile appeared on her face. She said, "He sat right where you are sitting every morning reading his newspaper and looking at his stock prices before he went to work. I enjoyed making him breakfast. We had a good life. He passed away a little over year ago now. I miss him. He was a good man. He never caused me any trouble."

I could hear Donette and Robert coming up the stairs carrying groceries. I thanked Dolly for the coffee and biscuits and went to help. This was the first of several coffee and baking powder biscuits on Saturday mornings with Dolly, and her great stories of Lead and Deadwood. I still remember the words she said and the love in her voice when she said them, "He was a good Man. He never caused me any trouble." I love you can be said in many languages and in many ways, even in stoic western.

We purchased a small house in Deadwood the hometown of the famous Wild Bill Hickock and Calamity Jane. It was a cute little story and a half house with beautiful views of the Black Hills from our front porch and only 2 miles down the mountain from the Homestake Clinic. It had wild red roses growing in the back yard. In the morning Donette and I would wake up to this wonderful aroma of wild roses floating delicately through our open windows. It was hard to start out the day badly with the house smelling of wild roses in the summer and waking up right next to the most important person in my life. In the winter we received a large amount of snow sometimes measured in feet not inches. The snow in the Black Hills is different than the heavy wet snow of the Midwest. It was light, fluffy and easy to walk though. There was no wind in the Black Hills where we lived. Even in heavy snow falls the snow would still delicately drift straight down and it was not unusual to have 5 or 6 inches sitting on top of a fence post. It was absolutely beautiful in the Black Hills, in winter, with the pure white snow decorating green boughs of the pine trees contrasting against the tans and red colors of the hills. We would put Robert and Bethany on a sled then Donette and I would pull them through the snow to a down town restaurant for supper or to a store for shopping. We looked like and could have been a Hallmark Christmas card or a Norman Rockwell painting. We had a great deal of fun in the snow.

Around Christmas we would go to the Forestry Office, purchase a permit for $1.50 that allowed us to go anywhere in the Black Hills Forest and cut down a Christmas Tree up to 20 feet tall. We had a small house and needed a small tree. Robert and I scoured the forest for some time until our attention was drawn to a small tree growing all alone out of a stone crack in the side of a cliff. We noticed this little tree in the huge forest because of a single random shaft of sunlight shining through a hole in the clouds that illuminated a small part of the cliff and that little tree. An unbelievable place for a single pine seed to fall, take root and grow. It was the right size about 6 feet tall and perfectly shaped until you looked at it from an angle. The whole back half of the tree, up against the cliff, had not grown and was missing. It was deformed. It would never be picked to be a Christmas Tree. We loved that incomplete little tree. Robert called it our Charley Brown Christmas tree. We took it home. Set it in a tree stand, watered it and slid it up against the wall. We decorated the tree and it looked as though half of the tree was inside the house and half outside. It was perfect for our little house. Everything has a place and a purpose, so this incomplete overlooked little tree became one of the most beautiful Christmas trees we have ever seen. If there are Christmas trees in Heaven, this one will be there.

Donette was much braver than I am. Working officially for the Homestake company, I and my family were encouraged to tour the mine. The powerful at the top of the company thought it would help us take better care of the miners, when they were brought into in the ER, if we saw the conditions in which they worked. I have a minor problem and It's with caves and tight places. I can't even watch TV shows where they are crawling through tight spaces underground. I declined their offer but Donette accepted. They ushered her and the other tour members into what they called an open lift but it should have been called an open fall. There was no roof, very little on any of the sides, and she stood on a wooden plank floor with nothing to hold onto except her neighbor. It was suspended by a single cable attached to the center of a steel bar above the tour members heads and the lift was large enough to hold up to twenty miners. Donette said, it felt like the floor dropped out from beneath her and it fell at 38 miles per hour for four thousand feet. The tour members grabbed each other's arms and clung on for stability. Out of the corner of her partially closed eyes, Donette could see the sides of the rock shaft race by as they fell. At the shaft bottom, they got onto a small mining train that went to another lift and dropped an additional four thousand feet at 38 miles per hour. Disney's tower of terror doesn't drop that fast or definitely not that far. They were eight thousand feet below the surface. The rock wall temperature was 110 degrees and this was where the mining began. The tour fascinated Donette, she loved it. A year and a half later, she went again. This time they had just started mining at the ten-thousand-foot level and she could see the gold run in streaks across the walls. A few weeks later, the miners were blasting in the mine to loosen the gold ore and blasted into the water table flooding parts of the mine. Amazingly no one was killed but a few miners were injured who were caught in the torrent of raging water racing through the mine slamming them against the shaft walls. They were brought into the ER where I took care of some of them. Donette decided against taking a third tour.

It truly was a western town. I was told that the gentleman who doubled several of the top cowboy movie stars lived locally. He was a six-shooter fast draw champion and had been in several well-known movies. On occasion he would give quick draw exhibitions at local bars using specially made soft wax bullets to hit targets. After each exhibition we would get a miner or a cowboy in the ER, who had a couple of drinks, and thought they could also be quick draw artists in the movies. Only to shoot themselves in the leg or foot with real bullets. The clinic took care of one person, who shot himself in the same leg twice, 6 months apart practicing his fast draw. He now had a limp to remind him that alcohol has never made anyone smarter or faster.

Sturgis South Dakota is just 13 miles down the mountain. One afternoon, during the Sturgis motorcycle week, a very rough tough looking motorcycle gang brought in one of their members with an obviously fractured right arm. They burst into the Hospital ER and took over. The older looking one with long hair said he was Dr so and so, but I'm sure he didn't give us his real name. He ordered an x-ray, set the fracture, put on a cast, then they left with no names, no address, and no insurance. Everyone in the ER breathed a sigh of relief and was very thankful they were gone. Two days later an ambulance brought in Dr so and so, who had crashed his motorcycle and suffered a fractured leg. It was found that he was wearing a long-haired wig and that he was indeed a doctor who was an orthopedic surgeon from California. He ordered them not to call his wife because she thinks he is in Las Vegas at a medical conference. Everyone was quite happy to ship him via ambulance to Rapid City for orthopedic surgery and let them deal with rest of the gang. I'm not sure how he is going to explain the fractured leg and the bills from South Dakota to his wife, it must have been a very rough conference. I was starting to get very concerned about raising our family here.

Donette became a teaching assistant at the Deadwood elementary school in first grade. She was a kind, warm, generous person who loved all children and the children loved her. Robert was in fourth grade at the same school. Bethany went next door to our neighbor's home for daycare. Donette detested violence and believed in kindness to all others. She taught this to our children and the children at school. Robert had a bully in his grade that had picked Rob out because he was the new kid. The bully was bigger than Rob and he would punch, push, shove or trip Robert every day at school. The school knew about this bully and either did nothing or couldn't stop him. Donette had talked to the principal about the bully and nothing was ever done. Robert hated going to school and would sometimes fake an illness to not go, just to avoid this person. I was too busy working in the ER and didn't know this was happening. No one ever mentioned it.

It became spring, Rob had just turned ten and school would be over in a few weeks. When I saw he had a torn shirt pocket and asked him how that happened, he told me the whole story. Rob said, "Dad I'm trying my very best not to hit him back. I've tried talking to him and it just gets worse." I remembered how I was bullied by two older high school boys when I was in Junior High and as a freshman in high school. I remembered how scared and angry it made me feel. One night, after leaving the movie theater on main street in Osage, they saw me. I was chased clear across town sprinting through people's backyards, hurdling over fences and through gardens in the dark until I reached home. One evening I was walking home from a high school football game. A car pulled up, stopped, two boys jumped out and yelled, "Get him." I was off and running again. I never felt completely safe outside of home and I felt humiliated whenever they were around. I was fed up. They had pushed me to the point where I didn't care what happened to me or them any longer. I had enough, I planted my feet, stood my ground and sought each one of them out individually. I found that bullies are cowards when they are alone and it's one on one. When confronted by a determined unafraid person, they backed down. I was angry that this was happening to our son. I told Rob that he is the only one who can actually stop the bullying. He needed to defend himself, to do what he thought was right to protect himself and we would stand by him. I trusted him.

The next day, at school, the bully shoved Robert down to the floor. Rob stood back up, clenched his fingers into a fist and punched the bully in the face laying him out flat on his back right in front of all the students in Robert's class. That evening, I noticed that the atmosphere at the supper table was different. It was lighter, happier and pleasant. Rob acted as if a weight had been taken off his shoulders. Donette told me about what had happened at school later that evening. I found out that the other kids were now standing up to the bully. It often takes someone to lead the way and sometimes kindness needs a little extra emphasis from a brave good person. Many times, this is what it takes to help the bully realize what it feels like to be on the receiving side and he didn't like it.

Our son and his friends from school wanted to play soccer because other surrounding towns had soccer teams and it looked like fun. It allowed kids not tall enough for basketball or big enough for football to enjoy a sport and boys and girls could both play. Donette started, with the help of other parents, The Lead-Deadwood Soccer League. She got teams organized, bought equipment and got concessions up and running at games. With a little time, much effort on her part, the league had money in the bank from the sales of concessions and was now self-supporting. The kids were having fun including the bully from Robert's class. He was still having a little trouble making friends, but he was being encouraged to be part of a team and he was working on it. Donette was very happy. Working with children made her day complete. I was so proud of her and loved her with all my heart.

In the summer, Deadwood was a wild west tourist town. In the winter, it was a ski resort. Every summer one of the attractions was a play entitled, "The Trial of Jack McCall. The low-down dirty scoundrel that shot Wild Bill in the back." The play started out at Saloon Number 10 on main street. Wild Bill was sitting at a table with his back to the bar playing poker. Jack McCall, who was drinking Red Eye at the bar quietly pulled out his large six shooter, referred to as a Hog Leg, shot Bill in the back and killed him. Then the play immediately proceeded out into the street as a gun fight, where Jack McCall ran out of bullets and surrendered to the sheriff. He was hauled off to jail and the play concluded that evening at the Deadwood Opera House.

My father came for a visit the last summer we lived there. We took him to all of the regular tourist attractions, showed him the clinic and ER where I worked and the school where Donette worked. We had started the day out at Saloon Number 10 and our tour concluded that evening at the Opera House for the finale of the play. It was my father, Donette, Robert, Bethany and myself. It was a packed house that evening but we found seats down in the front close to the stage. There weren't enough seats open for the five of us, so Bethany had to sit on my lap. The play was well done and quite enjoyable. There was a very dramatic moment after the prosecuting attorney laid out the case in front of the jury. He then turned to Jack McCall on the witness stand, angrily pointed his index finger at him and was about to accuse Jack of killing Wild Bill. At the very moment he pointed his finger, everyone in the opera house was holding their breath. It was so quiet we could have heard a pin drop outside the opera house. At the very instant he pointed his finger our three-year-old daughter, sitting on my lap, looked up at me and yelled loudly, "Dad, I got-a pee." I closed my eyes thinking this can't be real. This didn't just happen. Donette and Robert slowly slid down in their seats and leaned away from us as if they didn't know who we were. We were close enough to the stage that it brought the play to a halt. When a three-year-old has to go, you have to go now. I stood up and carried her up the entire length of the aisle amid a thunderous round of applause. Every embarrassing thing I have ever done to my mother came flooding into my brain. When I was five and we arrived home from doctor Huber's office, I had the mothers curse placed on me. My mother said, "When you grow up and have children, I hope they are just like you!" At the top of the opera house aisle, I turned, told Bethany to wave and she did her best royal impression to even more applause and cheers. After the bathroom, I bought our daughter a bag of popcorn. It was a beautiful summer evening in Deadwood. Perfect temperature, the air smelled of pine trees and an unbelievable canopy of stars could be seen overhead. We sat down outside the opera house on a wooden bench that was made out of a polished split log. As we waited for the rest of the family, the star of the show smiled with joy, scooted over next to me and offered to share her popcorn with her dad. My heart melted with love.

A Change Begins

While we lived in Deadwood, I became friends with a dentist who had a somewhat unpleasant personality. He believed that we lived, died and were dust, with no purpose or meaning. That we were just a random fluke of nature, nothing more, and nothing else. So, you had better have a good time now while you can because this is it. This is all there is. He believed in living life to the fullest of his ability and he did. Traveling, skiing, diving in the ocean or going wherever he wanted to go. One winter he and his wife were downhill skiing near Jackson Hole Wyoming. He was flying down the mountain too fast when he lost control of his skis', fell and broke his leg quite severely. The ski patrol rescued him, hauled him off the mountain to an awaiting ambulance and transported him to the hospital in Jackson Hole. The ER doctors promised they would make him comfortable and control his pain. His surgeon had the nurses put him in a quiet room at the far end of the hall where he could get some rest and they would plan on surgery for the next morning.

This was a hospital filled with seasoned professionals but somehow someone accidentally transposed the dose of narcotic pain medication and the time interval of dosing on his chart. He received double the dose in half the amount of time. The first dose was not a problem but the second or third would be highly dangerous. That evening his wife was planning to go to a well-known, highly recommended restaurant with family and friends for a relaxing evening. At the very last minute, something made her change her mind. She decided not to leave him, but to stay by his bedside and keep him company. After a dose of pain medication, he fell asleep. His wife decided to sit quietly and read her book. After a little while she noticed that he was not moving. She placed her hand on his upper arm and shook it with no response. It now appeared to her that he was not breathing, she screamed for the nurses and they came running.

He rose up out of his body and was floating next to the ceiling before his wife noticed he wasn't moving. He was confused because he saw what looked like him in the bed below, but it can't be him because he is him. He saw his wife sitting quietly reading her book next to what looked like him. Then a tunnel suddenly opened up above his right shoulder and he was sucked down the tunnel at lightning speed. He arrived at the other end and felt great with no pain. In his room the nurses had arrived and now started doing CPR. At the end of the tunnel, he was met by family members that had previously passed away and who were waiting for his arrival. Somehow, they knew he was coming. He had a wonderful conversation and visit with them until his uncle said, "I'm sorry, but you can't stay here. It's not your time yet. You have more to do." The nurses had figured out the error and injected intravenous Narcan, an Opioid blocker, that reverses the action of narcotic pain medication. He woke up in his body in pain. He had his surgery the next day, spent several days in the hospital and then was sent home to start rehab. I talked with him and his wife approximately six weeks later. He was still in a leg brace and on crutches, but I noticed he was different and had a completely different attitude. He smiled more and was actually pleasant. He told me his complete story and said, "There was a brilliant light at the end of the tunnel, and it's not a train, it's the people. They emit a glow around them, a radiant energy. I know people will think it was a hallucination, but I know it was real." His whole outlook on life had changed. He had even cracked a joke. He no longer believed that we lived, died and were dust, or that we were just some random flukes of nature. I'm not really sure what to make of this.

In the summer of 1982, the Homestake Gold Mine closed the clinic and its ER in a cost cutting move. I believe it was actually more in retribution than cost cutting. Cyanide and arsenic are used in the extraction of gold from the crushed and then pulverized rock ore. The clinic had forced the mine into spending over 2 million dollars installing a system that prevented the accidental overflow dumping of cyanide and arsenic into Whitewood creek. It came from the gold smelting plant and when the overflow went into the creek, the water would have a very strong aroma of almonds. The stream ran down the mountain through the city of Deadwood where children waded in the water. There was not a single living thing in that stream where the water smelled of almonds. It was crystal clear, pristine looking and deadly.

The Doctors, PAs, Nurses, Lab techs, Xray techs and secretaries were all out of a job. We were all scattered to different parts of the United States. I had already made plans on returning to the University of Iowa in September of that year for further training. On August 28th I had become drowsy, had a one vehicle serious accident that fractured my spine in three places and smashed my right collar bone. My right collar bone required surgery and a section of bone from the front of my right lower leg to rebuild it. We were without health insurance for only one month and of course that month was August. Our new insurance started in 4 days. I didn't have a job. We had no income. We went broke, lost everything and it was my fault.

It is not uncommon for people practicing medicine to think of themselves as something special and deserving of special treatment because of the work we do. I received a huge dose of reality and humility being placed on the receiving side of medicine. I was totally dependent on others for almost everything. On morning rounds doctors and nurses would come into my room and I would be talked about but not to. They would examine my wounds and then leave. Sometimes without saying a word to me. I was forced to lay flat on my back staring at the ceiling because of the back brace I was strapped into. Sometimes I couldn't even see them but I could hear them standing at the foot of the bed discussing my case. If I had a question, I would have to be quick to ask it before they rushed out of the room. I realized that I had been guilty of doing some of the very same things they were doing with the excuse that I was busy. I had the realization of how very impersonal that was and how my patients must have felt. I didn't like it. It made me feel as if I was some type medical experiment and not a person at all. I felt like an inanimate object being discussed. I was putting the future of my life and wellbeing in their hands. If medicine should be anything, it should be personal. Person to person. Human being to Human being. It was a compassionate profession that was becoming compassionless. I vowed from that moment on, when I entered a room to take care of a "person", I would sit down, look at them face to face and say;" How can I help you?" Everyone deserves special treatment.

I now know how women must have felt decades ago laced into those diabolical corsets. Mine was not called a corset. It was called a brace but it was the same thing. It went from under my chin to my pelvis and I was strapped in tight to hold my spine straight while it healed. It made breathing difficult and sneezing painful. I was not allowed to sit. I could only stand straight up or lay flat on my back for the next two months. Eating standing up was no problem but going to the bathroom was certainly interesting

After I was released from the hospital, we needed help and Donette's parents took us into their home in Osage. They had moved in a hospital bed and helped take care of me plus our family. They were wonderful people and I can't thank them enough. They were always there if we needed help. The word love was not foreign in their house as it was in my childhood home. When Donette's parents said it, it had meaning with feeling behind it and they said it often. Finally, in December, as Christmas approached, I was allowed to sit and ride in a car. One evening, Donette drove us around to look at everyone's Christmas lights. Bethany and Robert loved the lights and the anticipation of Christmas morning. Donette and I were very worried about Christmas because we had very little of anything. If it wasn't for Donette's parents and family, Christmas that year would have been very bleak and disappointing for Robert and Bethany. Their grandparents made sure they had presents under the tree on Christmas morning. Again, I can't thank them nearly enough. Family is everything.

I was bored out of my mind from not working and feeling guilty. Donette had taken a Job as a waitress in a local restaurant to help pay the bills. I needed to get back to work. I found a position advertised, in a medical journal in Lacrosse Wisconsin. In January I applied, interviewed and was accepted. It was a position with Gunderson Clinic and Lutheran Hospital in the Cardio Thoracic Surgery division. Donette, Robert, Bethany and I moved from her parents' home to an apartment in Holmen Wisconsin, just a few miles north of Lacrosse along the Mississippi River. This is where we started over again from nothing. The first day at work was the day I took my corset off and I threw it away. I neglected to mention that fact to my orthopedic surgeon whom I decided not to return to and get yelled at. We were broke, in debt and I needed to work. I became the assistant to a board certified Pediatric and Adult Cardio Thoracic surgeon. We became a team and operated together. I participated in over 2000 open heart surgeries, six years in Lacrosse and later six years in Madison Wisconsin. I actually stopped counting at 2000 so I don't know how many we actually performed. We operated on everyone from premature babies in trouble to people in their eighties in trouble. We never lost a child. I wish we could say that about adults. I noticed on occasion I would have a patient tell me very specifically what went on in the operating room. That couldn't happen, it was impossible. But it did happen. It didn't happen very often, but it wasn't rare either. After they were asleep, we taped their eyelids shut, placed headphones over their ears and played calming relaxing music because hearing is always the last sense to disappear in surgery. They also had enough anesthetic drugs in their system to put a horse to sleep. Yet, when I sat down to talk with them, they could tell me what we said, what we did, if we dropped an instrument and who was in the operating room. Some members of the team didn't come into the room until after the patient was completely asleep. They would tell me things that they could only know and describe if they actually saw them. One patient said, he was out of his body standing over in the corner watching his surgery. He was very specific and accurate about the details. I had heard a similar story before. This person triggered my memory of the older well liked white-haired doctor at the University of Iowa cafeteria, and my somewhat unpleasant now pleasant friend. I was taught in college a scientific materialistic view of life. If you can't see it, touch it, or measure it. It doesn't exist, but that doesn't explain what I am actually experiencing. The question becomes, do I believe and trust what I was told and taught or what the experiences are now showing me? I remembered the cloakroom in first grade, what those facts showed me, and the sneaky conniving nurse that I trusted who broke that trust. I now have begun to question what I was taught to believe. It is beginning to appear that the materialistic view of life may not be completely correct. There may be more to our existence than just this skin suit that we call us. "This above all, to thine own self be true." *-Polonius from Hamlet.-*

Things were starting to get better and we were getting bills paid off. We found and bought a lovely home on a corner lot in Holmen close to schools. Bethany and Robert could walk to school until Rob got his driver's license, then it became too far and they had to drive. Donette loves anything and everything romantic. She loves romantic movies, weddings, loves doing makeup and hair for prom and family weddings. She enjoyed it and it was fun for her. She loved just being part of the romance that happened on those occasions. So, she decided to apply to and entered cosmetology school in Lacrosse. She excels because of her artistic abilities and she is having fun. It's not work, it's fun for her. Donette in time earns a manager's license and takes a position managing a beauty shop for Bethany Riverside Senor living community. Our daughter's name may have helped her make the decision to take the job. She loved what she was doing. She loved working with grandmothers and grandfathers. She enjoyed listening to the stories of their lives and talking about their grandchildren. For many of them coming to her shop is the highlight of their day. Donette makes it fun. She receives many hugs and thanks for her kindness and attention. She loves this job.

After six years of working at Gunderson Clinic and Lutheran Hospital in Lacrosse, the Surgeon I was working with moved to Madison Wisconsin. I and my family were asked to please go along so he and I could continue working well together as a team at Meritor Hospital. I promised Donette that she could pick the place where we live if she would move. She agreed even though she would be giving up a job that she dearly loved. Her and Bethany searched the towns around Madison and found a small house in Mount Horeb. A very cute small town southwest of Madison surrounded by farms much like our hometown of Osage. It had a distinctive Norwegian and Swiss heritage. There were large carved wooden trolls from a local artist that lined main street and the town was locally known as Troll Town. Mount Horeb had a very picturesque down town with a main street that was lined with small shops that had unique items for sale and with restaurants that served Scandinavian cuisine that was wonderful. Donette and Bethany had made a perfect choice.

Rob had graduated and was out on his own before we moved. Bethany was now in high school as a freshman in Mount Horeb. She was the tallest person in her class in 8th grade and as a freshman. Other girls teased her constantly about her height. They would push her, shove her into lockers, and knock books out of her hands onto the floor. She was the new girl in town. Bullies are not confined to just one gender. One day at lunch in the cafeteria, one of the girls tried to tease her by rhyming mockingly out loud in front of everyone, "Gee your tall, do you play basketball?" Bethany had enough, she stood up, looked down on the other girl and said; "No, do you play miniature golf?" The students in the cafeteria burst into cheers and gave Bethany a standing ovation. Bethany never mentioned this, but I spoke at the school in health class on occasion and the principal told me the story. I was so proud of her brilliantly standing up for herself and no one mentioned her height ever again. She stopped growing that year and the boys in her class finally caught up.

During the time I worked for Meritor Hospital in Madison, Donette's brother's wife, Barbara, whom I jokingly called her and I the outlaws at family gatherings, developed a bowel obstruction. She was thin and rather frail at the time. She required urgent surgery and was transferred from the hospital in Osage Iowa to Rochester Minnesota where she underwent emergency surgery at Saint Mary's Hospital. It went well and she was recovering but on day five her blood pressure crashed. It went to almost nothing and she became unconscious. They rapidly pumped IV fluids into her veins to bring her plummeting blood pressure back up. They rushed her into the operating room thinking something had gone seriously wrong with the previous surgery inside the abdomen. They opened her abdomen and found nothing wrong. They found that it was an infection at an IV needle site in her arm that put germs into her blood stream. Then the germs rushed throughout her body and crashed her blood pressure which is called "sepsis" and produces septic shock.

Now because of all the IV fluids and handling of the delicate intestines, they had become so extremely swollen the surgeons could not close her thin abdomen completely. She was transferred to the intensive care unit on IV drugs to keep her blood pressure up. A ventilator to help her breath, IV antibiotics to fight the infection and sterile dressings over the partially open abdomen. The intestines were so swollen that they compressed and cut off their own blood supply. They had basically died and would have to be removed. On the following Sunday afternoon, the Doctors sat down with Barb's husband, children, Donette's sisters, Donette and I. Barb's parents had been delayed and arrived later. We were all devastated at the news. I had become the medical interpreter for the family. I knew there was no way she would possibly survive. The doctors told us that she would never be able to eat or drink again. She would require intravenous fluids and nutrition for the rest of her life. No one ever survives on just intravenous nutrition alone for very long. After much discussion and tears Barb's family asked the doctors to please turn the machines off, she would not want to live this way and they agreed.

I had to return to work the next day, so I left that afternoon and drove home. Donette stayed to help her brother and his family. My normal daily morning routine started with the clock radio playing music from a local radio station to wake me up. It's quite early in the morning, still dark and I would reach over to turn on the touch lamp on the bedside stand. I would get out of bed, walk down the hall to the living room and turn on the TV to channel 63 the business channel. I listened to the business news while getting ready for work in the morning. I was in a rut and had become a creature of habit. Having a routine is a way of avoiding making mistakes without ever having to think about what you're doing. On Tuesday morning the clock radio woke me up. I turned on the touch lamp. Walked down the hall, turned on the TV to channel 63 and went into the bathroom to shave. I started listening to the business news but when I turned on my electric razor the buzzing drowned out the sound from the TV. When I turned the razor off, I heard a choir singing. I went into the living room and the singing was coming from the television. It had changed from channel 63 to channel 76 by itself, the church channel, and there was a choir singing. I thought to myself, oh great we just bought this TV. Just then the power went off in the house. TV went off, bathroom lights went out, and the microwave clock went off. Now I'm worried something major was happening, but I could hear music coming from the bedroom and see light. I walked down the hall to where the music was playing, the touch lamp and clock radio were still on. Now I'm quite worried something is happening with the electricity in the house.

I turned off the clock radio and then the touch lamp. I tried to turn them back on but without success, they would not come back on no matter how many times I tried. As if they would miraculously turn on after the third or fourth try. Just then the phone in the bedroom rang, it was Donette, Barb had passed away earlier this morning. Instantly after hearing that the power returned. Was this just a coincidence, which I'm not sure I believe in any longer, or was Barb saying good bye? I have no explanation. None of that ever happened again.

After twelve years of cardio thoracic surgery working six years at Lutheran Hospital and six years at Meritor Hospital. At each I worked twelve days in a row to get two off. Seven out the twelve I was on call and at work because everything in this profession is an emergency. Many times, I would drive home at night and Donette would meet me at the back door with the phone in hand. It was the hospital. Someone was in trouble and I would have to return. If it was my weekend on call, I went to work on Friday morning and many times didn't get home until Monday night. Donette was essentially a single mother for those twelve years, because I was always at work. In my position I had literally and physically held over two thousand human hearts in my hands, had the stress of life and death every day and seldom got a full night of sleep. I was tired and exhausted. When I become overly stressed, I remain quiet and I don't talk. The stress was spilling over at home with Donette having to take care of everything. I was gradually losing my family. I missed almost everything our family did, birthdays, school plays, school concerts, holidays, almost everything. I had spent more of my life at work than with my family. Donette implored me to find something with regular hours so I could please be home. I thought this is what good dads did. We worked hard to provide for our families. To give them a good life. I had become so involved with work that I had forgotten that I was a part of their life and they were a part of mine. I also got caught up in the idea that if I wasn't at work taking care of people, they could die and it was taking its toll on my health. The stress was killing me and I couldn't see it, but Donette did. I am not sure at this point in our life that if I had been married to anyone else, would they have tolerated what we have been through and stayed with me? I had watched several colleagues' marriages fall apart with far less stress. One evening on the drive home I wished we could start over and I would change a few things. When I arrived home and Donette opened the door. I said to her, "Hi, my name is Les. Would you go with me to a drive-in theater on Friday night?" She hugged me and said, "I'd love too." If you are thinking at this point that Donette is an absolutely wonderful person, you would be right. Believe me, I knew how lucky I was. I loved Donette with all my heart.

I decided to take an urgent care position in Oregon Wisconsin, a suburb of Madison, for the next few years. It had regular hours and no weekends. I could spend more time with my family and I could get reacquainted with them. We actually had time to do some things. Bethany and I would meet Rob and go fishing together. If I was crawling around under the car fixing something, she would be under there with me learning. When she got her own car, Bethany could fix things herself and did. She installed a new stereo system in her car. I didn't know how to do that. The student now becomes the master.

Even though Donette wasn't working at this time, she had developed carpal tunnel syndrome in both of her wrists from the constant use of her hands sculpting hair for several years. It required surgery because her wrists had become so uncomfortably painful and her hands were becoming numb. She was losing feeling in her fingers from the carpal tunnel problem and would drop things like scissors or hot curling irons. After the surgery, she was told, no more hair dressing or the carpal tunnel syndrome could return and next time it may not be able to be corrected. She loved what she was doing, and had been thinking about opening up her own shop, but she didn't want the pain to come back. So, she went to work for the post office and became a postmaster of a very small one-person post office in a very small town.

The town of Gotham Wisconsin. No, Bruce Wayne did not live there, but they did have a bat cave. She made the post office the meeting spot for the town. She did landscaping, planted flowers and made it a beautiful place. It had a coffee pot, a candy dish for children and she set up a book exchange because the town had no library. The town loved their post office and her.

In November of 2005 I took a job in the ER at Grant Regional Health Center in Lancaster, Wisconsin. It also had regular hours and I could be home more. We bought a small house just 15 minutes from work. This house was a little closer to Donette's post office and she didn't have as far to drive. Working in a small town the pace is slower, more relaxed. You get to know most of the people that live there. They are your friends and neighbors, you get to know their families and children. There are advantages to this because you know who is doing what to whom or with whom. Sometimes courtesy of the town busybodies but you need to take that information with a large amount of skepticism. When certain persons came into the ER, the story they may be telling me is not the whole truth and nothing but the truth but I know them very well. I know how to take care of them accordingly. There are also times when no matter what we did, we couldn't save someone. Like a young boy that I knew. We tried for over an hour to save him after the ambulance brought him in. Until it became obvious it was of no use trying any longer. How do I tell the parents we did the very best we could and it failed. What words can I say to help a parent's broken heart. There are no words that would make this better. I wanted to walk out the door, go home, hug Donette and say I can't do this anymore. It really hurts. But I couldn't, because in the next room is someone depending on me. I have to regroup, pull myself together, wipe my face off and give them 100 per cent of my undivided attention. Some of us look at this as just a job. Just a way to make a living. Others avoid being personal, turn their emotions and feelings off to protect themselves. Some of us can't do that, so some turn to drugs or alcohol to reduce the stress and heart ache. Some get burned out and quit. I was fortunate. I had trained my brain to dump most of the memory of what I did each day in the ER. It started the moment I walked out of the Emergency Department door. By the time I arrived home the majority of what I had done that day was gone. It was the only way I could survive. I could walk in our door, smile at Donette, put my arms around her and not think of it again. I could just be home. That didn't always work all the time. There are still some people like the one I just mentioned that I remember to this day.

Love Never Dies

Donette and I had been married for a number of years at this point and I was working in the Emergency Department of Grant Regional hospital. She had never seen what I do. I think she still thought of me as that goofy young boy she married at age 19. Boys' brains don't fully develop until about age 25 and I had done a few silly things early on in our marriage. Like trying to buy an old Corvette and fix it up when we couldn't afford it. It's a very good thing that girls are more mature than boys at this age and she was able to stop me from doing the majority of those silly things, thank goodness. She occasionally would show me something on her skin or ask me a medical question. I would shift into my medical mind and give her an answer. She would say, "Oh, it is not." I would say; "then you should go see your doctor." It happened so often, I finally started just saying, "I don't know, why don't you go see your doctor and see what she says." But on occasion I would not be paying close attention again and would give her an answer. Then I would hear, "Oh, it is not."

Donette loved a program on television entitled "Medical Mysteries" One evening I arrived home from work and she had just sat down to watch it. I sat down with her and it was about 5 minutes into the program. There was a young man speaking and they were showing him from his shoulders on up. I said, "He has Wilson's disease. He can't metabolize copper." Donette looked at me with a scrunched-up face and said, "Yeah, right." meaning no. I said, "Yes, that's what he has." She didn't say anything further. The young man went on with his tale of woe about how he had been given the doctor shuffle, referred to multiple doctors and not one of them had a diagnosis. Finally at the end of the program in the last three minutes appeared the super-duper specialist to whom the young man had finally been referred. He said, "We came to the conclusion that this young man had the genetic inability to metabolize copper called Wilson's Disease." Donette turned toward me with a startled look of astonishment on her face. I said, "All they had to do was pay attention and actually look at this young man. He has a copper-colored ring in the colored part of his eye that is called a Kayser Fleischer ring and it's diagnostic. Then ask if any of his male relatives had mysteriously died in their 20s or 30s. That's all they had to do." Donette leaned back in her recliner. Whenever she gets deep in thought she becomes very quiet. She was very quiet for the rest of the evening hardly saying anything. It appeared that the world may have just abruptly changed. She was no longer married to that goofy 19-year-old that she thought she knew. When she got up to go to the kitchen, I stood up and I took her in my arms and said, "I love you sweetheart."

We had suddenly changed. Things became different. We became closer. She leaned her head against my chest and wrapped her arms around me. I don't remember her ever doing that before. This was more than just a hug. I think there was a time, in our marriage, when she thought she may have married the wrong person and a little bit of that lingering doubt had stayed in the back of her mind all of these years. Everything we have gone through over the years certainly wouldn't have alleviated that doubt. I could now see it in her face that she no longer thought that was the case. She never said, "Oh it is not" again. I truly loved her with all my heart.

Our kids are grown and married to two wonderful people. They have their own lives and careers. They have children and are very busy. It's just the two of us at home now and life was very good. We enjoyed being grandparents and being with each other. I enjoyed just being with Donette. I loved the smell of her perfume, the smell of cookies, cakes and sweet bread that she baked in the oven. On my birthday she would make me the most delicious German Chocolate cake you have ever tasted. The house smelled wonderful. Every Christmas she would spend a Saturday baking sweet bread, cookies and cakes. I was the official taste tester. That was the best job ever. They were wonderful.

I would come up behind her and put my arms around her waist. She would turn around with flour covered hands, smile, then put them on my cheeks and give me a kiss. I would have flour hand prints on both sides of my face and I would get the hint, she was busy. I was interrupting at a critical time of turning flour into art. The next day we would deliver them to our friends for Christmas. Every year our friends would look forward to this day and subtly ask, "Donette's baking this year for Christmas, isn't she?" The answer was always yes, to a sigh of relief or a "thank goodness."

I loved the little things we did together, going to a movie, going out for lunch. Putting the top down on the little car and driving to get an ice cream sundae. The simple things we enjoyed the most. I loved the touch of her soft hand in mine when we're walking and the sound of her voice. We held hands where ever we went and no one tried to push us apart. When she would get dressed up, she was so beautiful she would still make my heart pound and take my breath away. I would be tongue tied and say dumb things. Then I would say, "I'm sorry that's not what I meant." She would kiss my cheek and say, "I knew what you meant." I would still kick myself walking all the way down the hall. It seems some things never change. I often wished I could be as suave and romantic as those leading men in the romantic movies that Donette loved. I would have loved to have been as sophisticated as Cary Grant in an "Affair to Remember", or as romantic as Nicolas Cage in "City of Angels." I would have loved to have been like that for her if I could, but it was not meant to be. Years ago, someone wrote in a movie, "Love means never having to say you're sorry". That never made any sense. At least not to me. We all make mistakes, intentionally or unintentionally and you don't say "I'm sorry" to the one that means the most to you in the whole world. In real life that doesn't work as it shouldn't work. Love means asking for and giving forgiveness, putting their needs ahead of yours and sometimes letting go of the past to start again.

So, what happens when life is good and you relax. You let your guard down and just try to enjoy life. Life throws you a curve ball out of left field that you don't see coming and it blindsides you. It's not fair. It should have been me not her. Donette started to forget things that she had done all of her life. It gradually got worse to where we couldn't blame it on just getting a little older and Donette became scared. Then terrified. She knew something was very wrong and I didn't know how to help her.

We sought help from one of the best memory specialists in the United States. Donette was diagnosed with rapidly progressive Alzheimer's Disease. We went back and forth for routine checks on her condition and each time she would come out of the memory testing sobbing profusely because she had failed. The last time we went, Donette begged me to please not take her back there again. All the testing was doing was causing her pain and would not change the outcome. I did as she wished and we did not go back. In 2016 I retired to take care of Donette, because she could no longer stay alone. I was beginning to lose her and I knew it. She had been placed on Alzheimer's medications that in my opinion did almost nothing. Even if they did a little something, it would only make everyone's suffering longer. The medications didn't cure at most they just prolonged. Eventually you get to the point where you wish the suffering you are watching and the pain you are feeling would end. You just want the pain in your heart to go away. Then the guilt about feeling that way sets in, you become conflicted inside and angry at yourself for feeling that way. I have saved the lives of thousands of people, but I couldn't save the one life that meant the absolute world to me. I had promised to take care of her in sickness and in health. I felt like I had failed her. I loved her with all my heart.

On November 11th 2017 my father passed away from heart failure at the age of 92. He was thin, his mind was sharp, he walked a mile up and a mile back from home every day to get a cup of coffee and a newspaper. He still played drums and sang in a country and western band, but his heart had just worn out. He had survived World War II and cancer twice but at his age he could not survive this.

Several days after the funeral Donette and I were at home. Donette was sitting in the living room watching television. I was at the sink washing dishes that I could not put in the dishwasher. We had a double tub sink and I was working in the right side. Three weeks earlier our daughter and her family had been visiting at our home. She had accidentally left her tall gray stainless-steel travel mug behind. I washed it and placed it on the counter top in plain sight. So, when they came again, I would remember to give it back to them. It sat only 1 ½ feet to the left of the sink and had been sitting there untouched for 3 weeks. It suddenly flew across the countertop with such force that it bounced around inside the sink multiple times. I was startled and jumped backwards expecting the cupboard or something to have fallen off the wall sending the mug hurtling into the sink. There was nothing. Nothing had moved except the steel coffee mug. I stood there in absolute amazement for several minutes wondering how this could be. How could it be propelled with such force that it bounced around hitting all sides of the sink several times. Then it dawned on me what may have just happened. When people would ask my father as to what he attributed his longevity, he would answer, "Drink lots of coffee and don't worry." It would have been easy for me to write this off and say, "That was certainly interesting" and just leave it unexplained. As humans, we do that quite often. Except knowing what I know now what better way for my father to let me know he was around. He may have been trying to let me know he was around but I hadn't noticed. Sometimes I can be a bit dense, and as men we don't do hints well, but this certainly got my attention.

Before Donette became ill, because of her banking background and I was never home, she had taken care of all of our finances for years. We would get letters asking for donations around Christmas. Anything related to children such as Saint Jude's Hospital or Shriners Hospital for Children, she would send them a $50 check. So, every December we would get 10 to 12 calendars asking for donations. That December after my father passed away was no different, we were receiving calendars in the mail almost daily requesting donations from various organizations. This day, I retrieved the mail and it contained another large white cardboard envelope. I assumed it was another calendar, so I placed it on Donette's computer desk that she no longer was able to use. It sat there unnoticed for several days. One day I was listening to a streaming site on my computer called Pandora. The 60s and 70s era rock and roll while doing emails. I noticed the white cardboard envelope laying on her desk and decided to throw it away. We didn't need any more calendars, we had several. But before I threw it away, I decided I had better open it to make sure that it was a calendar. To my surprise it wasn't. It was a book, emerald green in color and with words embossed in gold lettering "Lift up Thine Eyes." At the bottom edge of the front cover also embossed in gold lettering it said, "In Memory Of" with my father's name. When I opened the cover of the book. It opened to a painting entitled the "Ascension." It was a painting of Christ ascending into Heaven. At the very moment I opened the book,

Pandora Radio played "Amazing Grace" sung by an Irish singer named Haley Westenra. That's hardly rock and roll. I could have written this off as maybe a coincidence except that my father's mother played piano for church services at their local church. She had an antique upright piano in her home, and when we went there for Thanksgiving Dinner or Christmas Dinner, she would sit down at the piano, play Amazing Grace and my father would sing. I was astonished.

Donette's Alzheimer's Disease, even on medication, continued to progress to the point where she didn't recognize me any longer. I had lost her and she had lost me. My heart was broken. I had taken care of her in our home 24/7 for over three and one half years, and I watched her as she slowly deteriorated right in front of my eyes. She now was hallucinating and seeing children playing in our home. Seeing children in our home would make her smile. Then she would become very upset and agitated when they wouldn't listen to her, in particular when she was trying to keep them safe from harm. She was having trouble eating. She couldn't remember or figure out how and needed help. It became obvious that I could no longer take care of her in our home. My health was starting to fail. I wasn't sleeping for fear she would get up in the night and fall down the stairs or wander outside. I had alarms on all of the outside doors but what if I didn't hear them. Our children convinced me that she needed to be in the group home that our Daughter-in-law owns and runs that is four hours' drive away in Eagan Minnesota. She would be taken care of by people that I knew would be kind, by doctors and nurses who could give her far better care than I could at this point. I was separated from her for the first time in 52 years and my heart ached. They started her on Seroquel, an antipsychotic drug, to stop the hallucinations and it worked. She went into the group home on May 2nd 2020 and passed away, exactly six months to the day later, on November 2nd 2020 with our daughter sitting by her side holding her hand. They had a very special bond between them. Bethany was Donette's miracle daughter.

Life had thrown me another curve ball. I had been exposed to Covid-19 and quarantined at home. I could not get a lousy Covid test for five days. The day I could finally get a covid test to see if I could be by her side, was the very day that Donette passed away just before I got the results. When I received the call from our daughter, I was four hours away and not with her. The guilt, the anguish and the feeling of loss were so overwhelming that I collapsed into a chair and just wanted to die. I knew this was coming, but we are never fully prepared for when it actually happens. I had never felt such pain and heartache in my entire life. A heart that is capable of feeling immense love is also capable of feeling immense pain. The Covid test was negative. I was angry and furious. How dare life does this to us. I never got the chance to say goodby and tell her how much I loved her. Being in medicine makes your brain sometimes think strange thoughts and I wondered if anyone had ever been so heartbroken that they died of dehydration from tears? I loved her with all the pieces of my shattered heart and I truly wanted to die. "What greater punishment is there than life, when you've lost everything that made it worth living?" *-William Shakespeare-*

My niece, Natashia is an extraordinary young woman. She is able to see, hear and speak with people who have passed away. She has been able to do so since she was 3 years old. I asked her recently, "Were you ever scared when you saw these people." She replied, "No, they were all nice and kind." She thought everyone could do this until she went to school and found out they couldn't. I'm guessing she was teased because she hid the gift away until in her early twenties when a Guardian Angel or what some call spirit guides came to her. He convinced her to use her gift and talent to heal people's hearts. I didn't know about this until almost 5 years ago, because she had also hidden it from family. Now she does Angel Readings upon request and connects people to their loved ones who have passed away. Tasha thinks doing this is no big deal. To her it's just a normal part of her life. She says my father, her grandfather, loves to drop by and change the music she's listening to. He changes it from the POP station to a country and western song just to let her know he dropped by, and does it fairly often. He loved his grandchildren.

Three weeks after Donette's grave side service, because that's all Covid restrictions would allow us to do, I was doing emails and whatever I could find to do on the computer just trying to occupy my mind. I just wanted the pain to go away. It was 9:30 in the evening when my phone rang. It was Tash. She said she was doing laundry and folding her two little girls' clothes when Donette appeared right next to her. She said Donette was young, had her black hair back, lipstick, ear rings and a beautiful white dress. She wanted Tash to call me and tell me, "Everything on the other side is real, that she is OK and very happy." She then showed Tash how she passed. She showed our daughter Bethany there holding Donette's hand as she passed. She showed Donette's mother, who had passed away years ago, placing one hand on Bethany's shoulder and the other outstretched to Donette and said, "Come with me." They went to where her father and the rest of the family were all joyfully and happily awaiting her arrival. Donette then turned away from Tash and when she turned back, Donette was holding a baby in her arms and had a big smile on her face. She was extremely happy. Donette loves all children and Tash is amazing. My heart was not as broken.

My children talked me into purchasing security cameras for our home hoping I would spend more time visiting them and not worrying about the house. So, I did. One for the kitchen facing the back door, one in the dining room facing the front door and one for the bedroom facing out the door into the hall. I think they were both afraid of losing me as they had just lost their mother. Afraid I would accidentally fall down the stairs with no one there, not eat or just sit down in a chair and waste away. I lied and reassured them that I was alright.

On Christmas Eve 2020 everyone had other places they needed to go. I was home alone having nowhere to go, and was having an unbelievably awful night. It was the first Christmas in 55 years that I wasn't with Donette. I felt incredibly alone and lonely. Sorrow and loss had taken over. I tried everything I could think of to occupy my mind. Absolutely nothing interested me. Every Christmas movie on TV was sad but at least had a happy ending. Nothing worked.

It was shortly after 11 o'clock in the evening and it certainly didn't feel like Christmas Eve. I was severely depressed and I decided that I would try going to bed. Maybe sleep would help although I hadn't slept more than a few hours each night for some time. I turned out the lights then suddenly in the dining room appeared orbs of light of various sizes. One the size of a soft ball and most of the others slightly larger than tennis balls flying randomly around the room. They were everywhere. I couldn't believe what I was seeing, but I knew what I was seeing. I was not alone. I recorded them on the security camera and have that on my phone to prove to myself that it was real. I would over analyze everything before we would buy something, I would research it to death. By the time I would get done, it was usually sold and Donette knew this. She knew I needed something that was indisputable. I love her with all my heart.

Still Photo from Security camera

Bethany and I went to Osage to see Tash and had an Angel Reading. We learned that Donette was in her life review and that she was back to her normal complete full self. That she was with family and very happy not to be ill. Donette told Tash that she saw me home alone on Christmas Eve so she sent me the lights and that she saw the donations to the Childrens hospitals that I sent in her name. I had not mentioned any of this to anyone. She confirmed it was her by saying that she heard me still saying good night and that I loved her before I go to sleep as I had done almost every night for the past 52 years. She said please don't be sad and that she would check in on me frequently. Tash told me that when you have a love connection to someone who has passed, talk to them, they will hear you. Then pay attention. If they think you are paying attention your loved ones are more likely to send you an answer.

Being home alone, the silence is unbearable at times when you are used to having family always around. So, I have a small black Bose speaker that is WIFI connected to the internet and controlled by my phone. I daily listen to a music streaming sight named Pandora to just have some sound in the house. One night while playing Pandora 60s and 70s rock and roll in the background on the speaker. I did what Tash told me to do. I spoke out loud to Donette about my fears that I had lost her. How much I missed her and that I was afraid that we may never be together again. I didn't know if or how she would respond and if I would even recognize it. In an instant the very next song that played on that speaker was not an old rock and roll song. It was a piano solo entitled "Soulmates" by Danny Wright. Wright was Donette's family name.

That could have been just a random coincidence crossed my mind, couldn't it? I was still very concerned that I may never see her again. A thought suddenly appeared in my mind, "If this is true and that song wasn't a coincidence. How would I ever find her in this vast endless universe?" Just then a song by the Irish group Clannad entitled "I Will Find You" played. (It just now started playing on Pandora at the very instant I finished typing the words "I will Find You".) This song is from the motion picture "The Last of The Mohicans." It has a special meaning to me, the main character's name is Hawkeye. I am a University of Iowa graduate. My nick name is Hawkeye.

Donette knows how I think and I can be quite skeptical. I Don't know how things are on the other side and I was worried that her feelings about me might have changed. So, I asked. The very next song "I Will

Always Love You" by Whitney Houston. Any doubt that I had disappeared.

I get chills and a wave of emotion that sweeps over my entire body when one of these special songs plays. It is a wave of emotion and a total body fine vibration that I cannot accurately describe but contains a knowing that the song was sent for me. That does not happen when these songs play and I haven't asked a question or it doesn't have some special purpose. Sometimes these songs that have a special meaning will even interrupt the song that is currently playing. Donette's younger sister's family invited me to the Childrens Christmas Program at Trinity Lutheran church which had been postponed into February 2021 due to covid-19. That was Donette's Family church and the church where we were married. I spoke out loud to Donette and told her about being invited to the Childrens Program and that she and her Mom and Dad should also attend. The very next song that interrupted what was currently playing on Pandora was a song entitled "We Will Meet You There." I got chills.

My father decided to join in. I'm working in the kitchen making lunch and listening to Pandora rock and roll. A song came on entitled "Nashville". I wasn't paying close attention and I thought ok, Pandora just wants to know if I like country and western music and if I will click the thumbs up button. I did not. Two days later, while making lunch, a song comes on entitled "Hillbilly Blood." Now I'm thinking, it's probably Dad. After what Tasha told me he does to her music. Two days later, at the same lunch time, "Cold, Cold Heart" sung by Norah

Jones but written and performed in the past by, Dad's favorite singer, Hank Williams played. Now I know it's my father. That was his favorite song and he would walk around the house unconsciously singing that song. He sang that song in the country and western band in which he played drums. I got the message. He had stopped by.

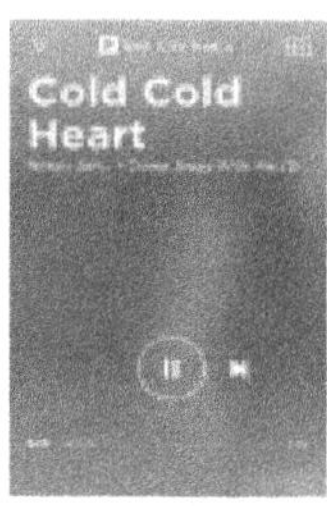

The other night I was working on my computer late. I said out loud "I'm really tired. I'm going to bed". At that very moment the song that played on Pandora was "Good Night My Angel" by the Celtic Women. I love you Donette with all my heart.

I purchase bananas from Kwik Trip frequently. Recently I purchased some that looked great. The peeled banana itself looked fine. I bit into it and down the center was black. It was awful. After seeing that, I choked, gagged and spit it out in the trash. I ranted and raved about the black center in the banana. At that very instant Pandora played "Day-O, The Banana Boat Song" by Harry Belafonte. I still buy bananas from Kwik Trip. Not one has had a black center. What is the random chance that I would choose the one banana at the exact time this song played? Not very likely. Donette had made me laugh. It had been a very long time since I had anything to laugh about.

I have collected pennies on and off for years. I would jokingly tell Donette that I was going to be a Penny Aire and have a million pennies. She would just look at me with the I don't think so look on her face. She was right, I only have a few. I recently went to the bank to deposit a check and asked the cashier for ten rolls of pennies. I took them home. Set them on the dining room table and forgot they were there. One day I had cleaned the house and had nothing left to do. I was bored and turned on pandora the 60s and 70s rock and roll I always play. I spotted the pennies and decided to go through them looking for any that were collectable. I sat down and the very instant I unrolled the first roll of pennies, Pandora played "Penny Lover" by Lionel Richie. It brought a smile to my face. I miss her immensely.

I play the Pandora station on the TV and listen to the music through the sound bar when I'm in the living room. I was sitting on the couch feeling particularly alone and lonely deeply missing Donette. The music had been playing for a short time when a song by the group

Foreigner played. "I Don't Want to Live Without You". After it played, the title and the album picture froze on the screen. The TV wasn't frozen because the album picture moved around the TV screen like a screen saver. The TV does not have the screen saver function. I watched it for several minutes and took a picture of what was on the screen with my phone. Another random coincidence? Not in my mind it wasn't. It has never happened before or since. It had a special meaning to me. I got chills.

Donette's Birthday is in March. The day before her birthday, I wasn't doing very well at all. I was already anticipating and dreading the next day. It would be the first time I wasn't with Donette on her birthday since we were 16 years old. I tried going to bed around 11 o'clock but I couldn't sleep. I knew the next day would be a very difficult day. It was then that the orbs of light suddenly appeared in the bedroom. It was an absolute blizzard of light flying around the room. They would pass right through the walls, and the door. I recorded them again and have that video on my phone. Donette's birthday was a good day, I knew I was not all alone.

Still Photo from Security camera

Just a few days ago I was watching motivational videos on YouTube. I had just finished watching a video by Matthew McConaughey and I wasn't paying very close attention, my mind was elsewhere. I couldn't tell you exactly what he said. The next one in line was Denzel Washington. I believe it was something about 10 things for a happier life. I thought I could certainly use a happier life. So, I put the curser on that video and clicked on it. That's not what played. What played was the 1968 video excerpt from William Shakespear's Romeo and Juliet. The song "A Time for Us." I love you Donette with all my heart.

On occasion I would find the 60s and 70s rock and roll changed to a station called "Owl City". It had a more diverse line up of music that was more in line with what Donette would like. It appears electronics are the easiest for those on the other side to manipulate. Moving things is harder it takes more energy but they do that also. I find my baseball cap moved to places I would never put it. When I mowed the lawn, I was wearing a white baseball cap to reflect the heat from the sun. After finishing, I went into the house and put the cap away in the computer room where I always place my caps. I went outside to get the mail from the mailbox and when I returned, I found my white baseball cap laying on the kitchen counter right next to and up against the butter dish. I would never put it next to the butter dish and get butter on the cap. Donette knows this. I knew she was there.

I took my mother and my aunt {my mother's sister} who both still lived in Osage, Iowa out for lunch at their favorite restaurant some time ago. While eating we started talking about this very subject and my aunt surprised me when she started talking about the day she died. She was at a local craft fair where the ambulance crew was showing off their new equipment. She stopped to watch and suddenly collapsed right in front of them. It took a few seconds for the startled crew to realize what had just happened before they sprang into action. They weren't expecting someone to suddenly drop-dead right in front of them. My aunt said she rose out of her body and was met by her mother, my grandmother. They stood there and watched as the paramedics started CPR, attached chest patches and shocked her. She turned to her mother to ask something and her mother turned to her, smiled and shook her head no as if she knew what question her daughter was about to ask. My aunt was slammed back into her body, opened her eyes and they stopped CPR. She was rushed in the ambulance to the hospital in Mason City, Iowa where she underwent two angioplasties with placement of two stents to open the arteries that supply blood to her heart. She said to my mother and I, "Mom doesn't have her gray hair anymore." She appeared slightly sad after that. My aunt's husband had passed away suddenly a few years ago. I didn't ask her what question she was about to ask, because I feel like I know what she wanted.

My daughter-in-law was driving down the highway with her teen age son beside her, our grandson, when an elderly woman pulled out in front of her and caused an accident. No one was injured seriously, they all got out of their cars, and were standing by the side of the road calling for help. My grandson realized he had left his cell phone in the wrecked car, went to retrieve it and was hit by another car. By someone not paying attention to their driving. He was launched through the air over the top of his terrified mother, landed in the middle of the hard concrete street, suffered a traumatic brain injury and back injuries. He was a brilliant student who was college bound, now his life had just been majorly upended and changed. After multiple failed therapies to ease the pain, his primary care doctor got him hooked on prescription narcotic medication trying to control his pain and then withdrew the medication because of a government crackdown on prescribing pain medication. My grandson, like many others who couldn't get their medication now, turned to his friends and classmates at school and they turned him on to street drugs to ease the pain. By the time he was in his early 20s he was in a downward spiral.

He had a very special relationship with his mother's father Tom, who passed away in 2018. The loss of his grandfather affected him very deeply. He also had a special relationship with his grandmother Donette, who passed away in November 2020. His best friend passed away last year from a serious health problem and all of this made his situation even worse. My grandson has had an intervention in the past and was taken to rehab. It did not succeed as most interventions don't when that person doesn't believe they need help. I asked him if I could take him to see Tasha for a reading. Maybe his grandfather would come through. It couldn't hurt to try. He agreed and said, "OK." In the reading with Tash, his grandfather Tom, grandmother Donette, and his best friend came through. They proved to him that it was them by telling him things that only he would know. Then they told him, that they knew and saw what he was going through. They knew his pain, his two Near Death Experiences that he never told anyone about and no one in our family knew of. We learned from Tom that when my grandson was hit by the car, four beings of light pulled his spirit out of his body before it slammed back onto the hard pavement. The beings of light communicated to him that he has more work to do on this earth helping others like him. That he must stay. His purpose in this life is to help others in the same situation that he's in. The only way to fully understand what someone else has gone through, is to have gone through it yourself. They promised him no pain if he went back and he had no pain for over an hour and a half after he returned. My grandson confirmed that all of this was true. He was afraid to tell anyone because he didn't understand what had just happened, so he couldn't imagine anyone else would either.

Tom told us about the second NDE from an accidental drug overdose that happened much later. Our grandson was in a city park with no one around. He was pulled out of his body by a male and a female appearing beings of light. They kept him from dying. They also communicated that he must stay as he has a future of helping others in trouble. At the time he didn't know how to interpret this and again never told anyone until now. His grandmother, Donette, told him she could see him in the future helping people who have gone through what he went through because he now understands. She communicated that she has been protecting him during these hard times, but the future is not written in stone and he must choose the right path. It is his choice which path he takes. They told him how they were trying to communicate with him but the drugs prevented him from seeing that communication. There was so much more that came through, but I can't put that in here now. He called me to tell me he is now paying attention and was seeing the communications. He feels his grandfather's hands on his arms and shoulders, and he would occasionally see balls of light swirling around him. Donette was good at doing that. Some of the NDEs when they come back are given a gift. The gift my grandson received was a photographic memory to offset the traumatic brain injury he suffered. He called to tell me that he had checked himself into a treatment facility that we know has success when you want to succeed. I recently talked with him again, he now has a job that he loves and is doing well. He has started working out, exercising again and has no intention of returning to his old life.

Random? I love my family with all my heart and I want all of them to do well.

Recently, I awoke very early and it was still completely dark outside. I had a very restless night tossing and turning all night. I missed Donette immensely. I turned on a light, went into the kitchen to get a drink of water and decided I might as well get dressed. It was of no use going back to bed, I was wide awake. I turned on the Bose speaker to listen to music while getting shaved and dressed. The first song that played was entitled "Thinking of You." The next two songs had the word Angel in their title and each meant something to me. The fourth song was Adele's song "Hello," with the lyrics "hello from the other side." After Adele's song played the speaker froze. No music played. The lights on the speaker were still turned on. It has never frozen before or since and I listen to it every day. I pushed a button on the top of the speaker and random songs began to play again as they normally do. A coincidence? A random occurrence? Again, I think not.

I have always been fascinated by history. Not the history taught in school, which were just names, dates and wars that we had to memorize then I would forget, but the real history stories. The complete stories about the real events and real people who lived them. Fallible people who made mistakes, did things wrong and got into trouble. People just like you and I. They were not superheroes. They were just ordinary people that found themselves in extraordinary circumstances and just like us, some succeeded and some did not. In the 1770s Daniel Boone was one of those. The colonists wanted to expand westward but the thick dense forests and mountain peaks of the Appalachian Mountains were in the way. They were an insurmountable barrier to westward migration. Daniel Boone was a pathfinder and trailblazer. A person who finds the way and then marks the trail for others to follow. He was recruited to find a pathway through to the west. Boone had made several attempts to find his way through and failed. But finally, Daniel Boone the pathfinder, found the way through. It became known as the Cumberland trail and Cumberland Gap.

I learned to navigate from my father and grandfather. I could use the Sun and time of day to tell direction. On a cloudy day when the Sun could not be seen, I knew that moss always grows on the north side of trees, that flowers and plants point southward toward the sun. I always knew where North, South, East and West were. The Moon, Big Dipper, and North Star were my guides to navigate the deepest darkest woods at night and I never got lost carrying those raccoons back to the car in the dark. When Donette and I would travel, she always had a map and wanted me to use it. I would tell her that I would get us close to our destination and then we would use the map. I would tease her by saying, "I am Hawkeye the Pathfinder." One Sunday in August, a few years after we were married but before our daughter was born, we were driving to a 50th Wedding Anniversary celebration in Iowa at a small church out in the country. It was small rural church, in a park like setting surrounded by tall trees and rows of flowers, but it was all alone out in the middle of nowhere. We had been driving for some time, with Robert in the back seat and Donette in the passenger's seat holding a map. Donette asked, "We're lost, aren't we?" I said, "No." Donette sarcastically replied, "Oh yes, I forgot. You're the pathfinder. Do you know where we are?" I said, "Yes, generally, sort of." She asked, "Do you want to look at the map?" I said, "No, I'm driving. Did Daniel Boone or Davy Crockett have a map?" Donette replied, "No, but they weren't driving a Ford Taurus looking for a church in Iowa and going to be late. We're not going to be there on time, are we? We're lost." I said, "I know exactly where we are. It's right there" as I breathed a sigh of relief and pointed to the church in the park. Donette looked up from the map and glanced at her watch then said, "Oh, good. We're just few minutes late."

Later when we were all alone, outside walking in the park looking at the rows of flowers, I took her in my arms and I admitted, "For a short while, we were actually lost. I didn't really know where we were. I just couldn't admit it, and it was mostly luck that I found the church. Foolish pride, I guess and I'm sorry. If I have to be lost, I can't think of a single person I'd rather be lost with more than you." She smiled, kissed me and said, "Me too." On the way home, I asked her to read the map and be our navigator. We arrived home in at least thirty minutes less time than traveling to the celebration. From then on, I was the Pathfinder when we were on a lake, at the state park or in the wilderness. In the car and on the road traveling, she was our navigator for the rest of our life. I certainly miss my navigator immensely.

In March of 2022, I started finding quarters around the house in plain sight. I had just vacuumed the floor, put the vacuum away and then returned to find a quarter in plain sight right in the middle of the living room floor. Over the next few days, I found them on the couch, on the dining room table, in the middle of the kitchen floor and elsewhere. I use a debit or a credit card so I don't receive change any longer, and I haven't for some time. I do collect pennies, but I get them in rolls from the bank. If I would have found pennies, I wouldn't have thought anything of it. I began to suspect what was happening but I could have been easily convinced otherwise, until I found a quarter on Donette's bedside stand. I had dusted Donette's bedside stand many times since she had passed away and there was no quarter. This quarter was shiny and new laying in plain sight next to her lamp. It was a commemorative quarter with the picture side facing up. When I saw what it was, it took my breath away and made my heart pound. I had to sit down on the bed before my legs buckled beneath me and I fell down. It was the Cumberland Gap commemorative quarter with Daniel Boone facing west holding his flintlock rifle and the date on the quarter was 2016. The year that Hawkeye the Pathfinder retired to take care of his Navigator. Just as I finished typing the word Navigator, Pandora played "I Will Find You" the theme from the Last of The Mohicans. Very interesting timing.

Donette's middle name is Rose. Her favorite flowers were roses of any color as long as they had the sweet smell of the wild roses that were growing outside of our bedroom window in Deadwood. The light Black Hills summer breeze, that worked its way down through the canyons, would pick up the aroma and carry it through our open bedroom window to throughout the entire house making it smell wonderful. For that aroma to be present, real roses must be grown outside in nature, but we had a late spring this year and nothing was blooming. Hot house or green house roses do not smell as sweet as those that are allowed to grow free and they last for such a disappointingly short time. Memorial Day would be here in just a few days, so I bought eight bright red and four snow white silk roses. I arranged the dozen roses with their green petaled stems that I inserted into a Styrofoam frog to hold them securely inside the vase on windy days. On Sunday, the day before Memorial Day, I placed them on

Donette's grave and sprinkled the center of each silk rose with several drops from a tiny bottle of 5% Rose Oil. The soft breeze carried the rose scent into the air and it was almost intoxicating. It triggered a flood of emotions and memories that caused the overflow from those memories to run down both of my cheeks which I wiped quickly away before anyone would see.

On Memorial Day, I awoke at 4am. Holidays are difficult when what made them joyful is gone. I was home alone, 3 hours away from Donette's grave with the silk flowers in Osage. I spent the day doing meaningless and insignificant tasks to keep occupied. Late in the afternoon I sat down on the couch in my usual well-worn spot to watch television. I had just turned the television on when suddenly the living room was filled with the unmistakable scent of wild roses. It lasted approximately 60 seconds and was gone. I frantically searched the house for a plausible possible cause and explanation. I looked on the front and back porches to see if anyone had delivered a bouquet of fresh roses. There were no roses. There were none in the neighborhood let alone any that were blooming. The scent was gone and nowhere to be found. I started second guessing myself and said out load, "It's Memorial Day. I must have been imagining it." I reluctantly returned to the living room and before I could sit down, it happened again. This time there was no doubt. It brought a smile to my face and Joy to my heart. I didn't have to look any further. If love has a scent, this would be it. I love you with all my heart.

I have multiple examples. Way too many to list. If it was just one or even a few examples, a skeptic would just write it off. It's hard to write off when I see it with my own eyes, hear it with my own ears and have it on video. How many times does something have to happen before you notice. Have you seen something in your life you couldn't explain and just let it go. When it may have been someone you lost letting you know they dropped by. Tasha said, "If you have a love connection to someone, talk to them, they will hear you." Donette said, "Don't be sad," that she would check in on me frequently and she does.

One last example. Some friends of ours gave us a memorial bench dedicated to Donette after she passed away. It has a saying carved into the seat that reads, "Our Family Chain is broken and nothing seems the same, but as God calls us one by one the Chain will link again." It sits on the north side of the house in the flower and rock garden. I purchased a total of eight solar lighted "Bright Pink" silk roses. I placed one on Donette's grave and one beside each end of the bench. The other five are on the east side of the house facing the sunrise. The bench and the two roses are in sunlight until around 10 am in the morning and then are in cool shade for the rest of the day. The others are in sunshine most of or all of the day. One evening three days after I had placed the pink roses, I thought that I should check to make sure they were actually lighting up at night. That night I found all of the lighted roses were shining brightly, but to my astonishment the rose on each end of the bench had turned absolutely pure white. Not even a hint of pink anywhere. The other five remained bright pink. Ordinary small miracles really do happen.

There is very little on regular television worth watching right now. I was watching a few YouTube videos when I accidentally came across a video of Doctor Bruce Greyson from the University of Virginia and he was discussing his research into NDEs, Near Death Experiences. The very subject that I knew something about but could not discuss in the past and keep my job. He stated that between 10% to 20% of people that have heart surgery, a major heart attack or cardiac arrest where the heart stops beating, will have a Near Death Experience where they leave their body and go elsewhere. They are met by family that have passed before them or by beings of light. True for my aunt, grandson and my unpleasant friend. In open heart surgery, it has been a subject that is not talked about or even mentioned if you want to keep your position but is now well known. I think most people who have been patients won't mention it, because of their fear that we will think they are crazy. It appears that very scenario seems to have happened. There have been cases of what now appear to be classic NDEs that have ended up in psychiatric units, on drugs, because their doctor didn't understand what the patient was talking about. It's that materialist view of life again. If you can't see it, touch it or measure it. It doesn't exist. Whenever one of our Open-Heart patients would talk to me about this subject, the conversation always started with, "You're going to think I'm crazy." At first, like everyone else, I thought it was the drugs that we administer causing hallucinations, but that couldn't explain how extremely accurate and detailed they were with their descriptions. Including what we said in the OR. No one can hallucinate someone else's conversation. It's impossible. It has now been proven by studies not to be the drugs.

According to Doctor Greyson, the NDEs are told they are not done yet and need to return to complete their life, they have more to do. This was true of my grandson and my somewhat unpleasant now pleasant friend. A few are given a choice to return or not, then shown their life if they return and the lives of others around them if they don't. Most of them shown this decide to return. We had an open-heart surgery case of a 52-year-old avid runner. Who didn't smoke, drink or take drugs. He had a very successful professional but stressful career and was in excellent health. Except for one single partial blockage in the left main coronary artery of his heart. This type of blockage was also known as the "Widow Maker." Men would just suddenly drop dead with little to no warning. The warning this person had was not being able to run quite as far before he became very short of breath and the distance was becoming shorter each time. His heart needed a two-vessel bypass to save his life. The heart was kept very still during the actual surgery with medication and the procedure went very smoothly. We were done with the two-vessel bypass in less than an hour and a half because everything went so well. We were ready to come off the heart lung bypass machine that maintained blood pressure and oxygen by pumping blood throughout his entire body but his heart would not start. We administered medications to start his heart and nothing happened. We tried different medications. The surgeon shocked his heart and still nothing happened. We attached a pacemaker directly to his heart muscle and no movement at all. Only a minor quiver where the pacemaker wires were attached. We tried a different pacemaker and still nothing. We tried for hours to start his heart until it became fruitless to try any longer. We had never seen a heart that remained this still. I left the operating room and sat down with his family and friends. I explained the entire situation to everyone and the only person in that room that was shocked was me. I was amazed by their lack of emotion. Suddenly the tables had turned and I was the one being explained to. His wife looked down towards the floor and sighed. Another family member explained, that last evening, he told them that he knew he wasn't going to make it through the surgery. He had his will, finances and all of his affairs in order. He had everything arranged for them and they couldn't talk him out of this. He was determined to go through with the surgery and that was the way he wanted it. I didn't know then what I believe now. My rather unpleasant friend described the people at the end of the tunnel as radiating a glow around them. An energy. The spirit, the soul or whatever you want to call it. Your radiant pure energy self is the power source that drives your everything. It makes everything move. Without it nothing works. I now believe that this person was one of the few that chose to leave and not return. We are so incredibly more than this powerless shell we leave behind.

Doctor Greyson and other experts say there are over 1 million NDE cases in just the United States alone. Some NDEs are shown a life review from birth to current time. I am told that during the life review you not only go through it from your perspective but through the eyes and feelings of those you affected both directly and indirectly. It can be happy, joyful, painful, terrifying and more depending on how you treated others. When Bethany and I had the Angel reading with Tash we were told Donette was in her life review. I can't imagine Her's being anything but joyful for someone so kind. So, in the end it doesn't matter what your bank account says, what house you live in or your job title. Those things are certainly very nice, they make life here on earth more pleasant but they are just temporary and don't actually matter. They are unimportant in your life review. It doesn't matter how famous or important you were. The only things that really matter are honesty, integrity, the kindness that you showed and how you treated those around you. It's quite simple.

I still remember that booming voice inside my head when I was 10, it said, "You can live without love." I never heard that voice again and I still don't know where it came from, but it had to come from somewhere. Was that the reason I was here? To learn what unconditional love was. As a child, for some strange reason, even though I was part of a family, I felt lonely at times. Like something was missing. When I found Donette I didn't know what love was. That word was never even mentioned in my family. It took me a life time to understand what that word meant, and I had to lose the most important person in my life to fully realize it. With her I discovered that love was the most wonderful amazing feeling that permeated every fiber of my being and I cannot imagine now living without her or without it. The answer is yes, you can be alive without love but it's not really living. You get to decide whether or not it's worth being that way and with free will you get to choose which path you take. Without love it's a very lonely way to exist and existing is the proper word instead of living. I imagine a lot of us these days are just existing instead of living. Life has definitely changed and is more difficult now than when we were young. Too many people in this world are existing in fear of everything. We somehow need to find faith in ourselves again, discover what living and loving really are, and then see where it goes. No one will do it for you. It's up to you. It's your life, you own it. It is amazing to me that you can change the word Living to Loving and all it takes is a simple I change. It's our choice to live in love or exist in fear.

When Shakespeare wrote "All the world's a stage, and all the men and women merely players," those may have been the most prophetic words ever written. This earth may be our stage for this loosely scripted improvisational performance but it is not our home. Ask the NDEs how they felt on the other side and they all consistently reply "I felt like I was home." When you look in the mirror, what you see is not who you really are. It is merely the costume you wear for this performance. We are here playing a part to teach someone something, to help someone or for us to learn something. How can you know what joy really is without knowing sorrow. What love is without knowing the absence of it. Each of the major events in my life taught me something. I learned what love is. What humility was. What kindness and compassion are. The pain of loss, sadness and sorrow. I've also learned how to save lives and fix cars except for the Valiant. Was all of that just random?

We become the product of what we are told and taught by our parents and the ones who came before us in what we believe to be true and important. That was certainly the case when I was in college. I studied constantly at home, in the car, on the bus and I worked very hard. I was materialistic and I wanted to succeed. If we have only one life, I wanted the big house, the luxury car and the comfortable life style. I was taught and told that having those was what success was and I believed them. I wanted that for my family. I wanted them to have a great life and to enjoy it. I wanted the best for them but it didn't happen, or at least I thought it didn't, but maybe the best actually did happen. Those things all seem so unimportant now. I look back at my life and I am amazed. It was certainly not the materialistic life I imagined it would be when I was young. I was determined to show those who teased me in my childhood what a success was, but I did not become the great wealthy scientist. I'm glad that didn't happen. I would have missed out on so much of real life. Real honest to goodness real life with real down to earth people that I met every day who lived vastly different lives. I learned so much about what was really important, but it took me a lifetime to do so. I will consider my life a success if after I am gone someone can honestly and truly say, "The world was a little better place for a while because he was in it." Then I will have succeeded.

I look back at Donette's life and I am so very thankful that she let me be a part of it. That she tolerated my dragging her and our family all over the Midwest. Even with all of our moves she did a great many things, accomplished a great deal in her short life and it always involved kindness and love. Wherever she went Donette carried those values with her. Those principles are infectious. A simple smile, a kind word, and a compassionate ear do wonders. They affected everyone near her, myself included. Donette taught me that the simplest gesture of kindness towards another, may ripple outward from that person like a pebble dropped into a still pond that will roll out in waves to affect many. Enough ripples can make the world a much nicer place. I loved those little houses we had that Donette decorated so beautifully. They were so cozy, warm and comfortable. I will never forget that wonderfully deformed little Christmas Tree, that was illuminated by a single shaft of sunlight, that Donette decorated so magnificently. She made each one of those houses feel like home. It occurred to me that I could live anywhere as long as Donette was there. Wherever she was, that was my home no matter where it was. If she was there, I was home. A house is constructed out of brick, wood and plaster, but a home is made out of love. This world, without a doubt, was certainly a little better place for a while because she was in it. I love her with all my heart.

I am not the same person I was when I graduated from college. Life is a difficult journey with many twists, turns and surprises. Each with its own purpose. Even when it's hard to see what that purpose may be when you are experiencing it. Look at my grandson who was gaining understanding, my rather unpleasant friend who was on what appeared to be the wrong path, the anatomy student that I still don't understand and the events in my life. Many of those were considered disasters. The very serious accident, that I thought was a horrific disaster, changed my life completely. It changed my point of view and sent me in a whole new direction where I met people that told me incredible stories. It was a path that got me to where I am now. What if Donette's father hadn't come back from the war, my father hadn't been transferred off of his original ship or the torpedo hadn't veered off. If we hadn't moved back from California or Donette's car didn't break down. What if we hadn't moved to the Black Hills where the change began? Were those all merely a coincidence? A random chance? Or is there some design? If even one of those hadn't happened this story would have never been lived or told. The picture of our grandchildren at the beginning of this story would never have been taken. Their lives may never have existed. Look at the people who have come into and out of your life so far and how they affected it both good and bad. Was that random? Did you learn something, help someone, teach someone something? Did you change someone's life or did they change yours? Was my meeting Donette totally random? When we see someone and feel like we know them but have never met them. It's because we seem to have some sort of an inexplicable connection that draws us to them. Like we've known them before and are seeing them again. I had that feeling whenever I was close to Donette. I couldn't explain it then, but it seems perfectly obvious to me now. It's uncanny how something, someone, or whatever name you want it to have kept making sure that we bumped into each other at the most opportune moments in our lives. To make absolutely certain that we would be together. It makes complete sense to me now as to the reason why the first song she sent me was "soulmates."

Like an ex-smoker or an ex-alcoholic who wants to tell everyone to quit smoking or drinking, I am an ex-materialist that wants you to know that I am now thoroughly convinced beyond a shadow of a doubt that no one ever actually ceases to exist. When I asked, "What happens when we die?" and my father replied, "I don't know. No one has ever come back to tell us." That appears not to be the case any longer. I am not sure exactly what we are, but we are definitely not some random flukes of nature. Life wonderfully does go on elsewhere and I am comforted by the fact that it appears we get to take what we have learned plus all of the love we have in our hearts with us.

The ending to Donette's and my life story has not been written yet and maybe it never will be. Maybe it just continues on with a new chapter when I see her again, take her in my arms, tell her how much I love her and we are together once again. Where ever She is, that is my home.

"I love thee with a love that shall never die,
till the sun grows cold and the stars grow old."
-William Shakespeare-

PS: Tasha tells me that Donette comes through now with an Angelic energy and that she is taking care of children in Heaven. No surprise for someone so kind, who loves all children.

Donette and Grandson
"True Love cannot be found
where it does not exist,
Nor can it be hidden
Where it truly does."
-William Shakespeare-
Not All Angels Have Wings
I love this angel with all my heart.
Les

To see the 3 videos that were mentioned in the book. Go to Youtube and search, or Google "A Random Life Love Never Dies" for the 5 minute video.